So You Think Your Business Needs a Computer?

Khalid Aziz

Copyright © Khalid Aziz 1986

All rights reserved

First published in Great Britain in 1986
by Kogan Page Ltd, 120 Pentonville Road,
London N1 9JN

British Library Cataloguing in Publication Data
Aziz, Khalid, *1953—*
  So you think your business needs a computer?
  1. Business — Data processing
  I. Title
  658′.05   HF5548.2

  ISBN 0-85038-998-4

Printed and bound in Great Britain by Biddles Ltd.,
Guildford

Foreword

by David Trippier, RD, JP, MP, Parliamentary Under-Secretary of State for Employment

There are more micros — home computers, personal computers and workstations — in Britain than anywhere else in Europe.

Already there is at least one microcomputer in every school in Britain and by 1987, it has been estimated, half of all British households will have a micro, compared with an expected 25 per cent of German and only 15 per cent of French households.

In our factories and workshops microelectronics are making computer aided design and manufacturing systems even cheaper, more compact and simpler to operate. They are now within the reach of many small manufacturers.

The pace of change is quickening, too, in the office. Voice, text, picture or data, whatever the information, can now be processed, stored, retrieved, displayed and communicated entirely in electronic form. With the automated office becoming not only quicker and more reliable, but cheaper too, it is easier now than ever before for the small businessman's office to be as productive and effective as the rest of his enterprise.

Choosing what is the most suitable and most cost-effective equipment is, however, a daunting task. Small businessmen contemplating the purchase of a computer system need all the advice and guidance they can get to help them make the right decision and this book sets out to give it to them in a straightforward, user-friendly way.

Contents

Foreword
by David Trippier, RD, JP, MP, Parliamentary Under-Secretary of State for Trade and Industry 3

Introduction 9

1. Why Do You Want a Computer? 11

The accounting miracle 12; Stock control 13; Plan to meet your financial fate 13; A wonderful way with words 14; File it 17; Work expands to meet capacity 17; Checklist 18; Case study: Overcoming fears 18

2. Who Will Use the Computer? 21

Power to the people? 22; How much knowledge 23; How many people should be involved? 24; Consultation cures criticism 25; Talking takes time 27; Summary 29; Case study: Training 30

3. Can You Really Afford a Computer? 31

Hardware 31; Software 32; The cost of thought 34; Matching systems and software 36; Kennelling the computer 40; Computer stationery 41; Ribbons 42; Maintenance 42; All data, no information! 43; Preventing loss of data 43; Plan for the future 44; A better way 45; Case study: Polymedia 46

4. The Computer Salesman 48

High street retailers 48; Finding the right dealer 51; How big is their byte? 53; Come, see, conquer! 56; Deal yourself a good hand 57; A better way? 59; The computer contract 59

5. Software First   61

The software consultant's role 62; Who are these consultants? 62; Consultancies 65; Recommended consultants 66; Who needs a consultant? 67; Measure their mettle 68; The price is right? 71; Reducing software costs 72; The hard choice 74; Training and maintenance 76; The long term 78; Case Study: Olive Tree Trading Company 79

6. Getting Down to Basics   82

Storage 82; Documentation 85; The costs 88

7. Spreadsheets   91

Using a spreadsheet 91; Choosing spreadsheet software 94; Spreadsheet operation 95; Other uses 95; Case study: Bournemouth Business Link 96

8. Word Processing   98

What should the package do for you? 98; What you see is what you get 99; Print and edit simultaneously 100; Fast formatting 100; Block ranging 101; Bold 101; Hunt, search and replace 102; Taken for granted 103; Help! 104; Spelling it out 105

9. Keeping Accounts   108

Sales and invoicing 108; Stock control 110; Stay on target 112; Allow for growth 113; Security 114; Conclusion 114

10. Filing   116

Introduction 116; Enter the database! 117; Database capacity 118; Formatting the entries 118; Printed data 120; Explore the potential 120

11. Computing the Payroll   122

Keeping up to date 122; Running time 123; Summary 124

12. Graphics —— 125
Bar charts 125; Alternative graphic representations 126; Software packages 126; Colour 127; Sharpening up the image 127; Summary 128

13. Getting the Message —— 129
Messages within the company 129; Distance messaging 132; Costs 134

14. Software — the Next Step —— 135
Specialist packages 136; Case study: RJL Software 136

15. The Hardware —— 139
Micro computers 139; The central processor 140; Keyboards 143; Screening it 146; Disk drives 148; Disk storage 150; Case study: the second-hand option 150

16. Peripherals —— 153
Printers 153; Modems 158; Joysticks and light pens 160; Bar code readers 161; Future developments 161

17. Installation —— 162
Power supply 162; The computer's ideal home 162; Men and machines 163; People first 164; Making room 165; The purchase agreement 167; The final touches 168; Checklist 170

18. Past, Present and Future? —— 171
Home computers 171; Business computers 171; Bigger, better? 172; Friendlier 172; Smarter 173; Over to you 175

Appendices —— 177
1. Where to Go for Advice —— 179
2. The Data Protection Act —— 182
3. Glossary —— 183

Index —— 188

Introduction

This is not a book about computers. It is really about people, because whatever you may have been told about computer technology, computers can only be as good as the people they serve. Not that you would gain that impression when talking to some of the new and ever-growing breed of computer buffs. Hand in hand with the best and smartest advertising agencies money can buy these computercrats are responsible for more misleading copy about their precious machines than most people could credit. The majority are not easily hoodwinked, however; perhaps once bitten by computers past, they have coined alternative definitions of the computer age: 'Computers are only good at providing solutions in search of problems' and, 'A computer is a device designed to give the businessman information he does not need, at a price he cannot afford,' are just two.

I have much sympathy with the underlying views expressed in those verdicts. It is true that computers have made great strides; they are, to be sure, now more 'user friendly'. But why were they offered to the public when they were presumably 'user *un*friendly'? Imagine someone trying to market a similar piece of complicated equipment (a car, for example) similarly inimical, to an unsuspecting populace. No, the time has come for the customers to stop being imposed upon by the computer industry by making sure that we get from computers what *we* require and not what the computer salesman wants to offer us.

This book will help you to formulate your ideas about computers and how they could fit in to your business life. It is primarily aimed at those looking for a computer for business purposes, but given time, computers will have growing relevance on the domestic front and increasingly be used for much more than whiling away vast hours playing outlandish video games.

I am not a computer expert, but in the couple of years leading up to the writing of this book, I have learnt a lot about computers from practical experience. At the same time I have retained a healthy scepticism about their abilities. I believe, therefore, that

So You Think Your Business Needs a Computer?

when you read this you will see that I have tackled the subject from your point of view even though I may have picked up some of the jargon. I am sure that computers have a great deal to offer many people. But not all computers, and not all people. Despite what the computer industry says, the choice is still ours, and we can always say no.

Chapter 1

Why Do You Want a Computer?

Here you are quite literally minding your own business and suddenly you get the urge to bring in a computer. Why? After all, hasn't the business been running well, generating profits, providing a good income for yourself and your work-force, laying the foundations of a secure future? It hasn't? Then you probably cannot afford a computer anyway (see Chapter 3).

Let us assume that you are in profit or at least running according to the budgets laid down in your business plan. You have probably heard about computers and their capabilities. You will also have heard that the computer today is streets ahead of what it was just months ago. You will have heard too that computers can be a nightmare, bringing businesses to a virtual standstill, rendering otherwise amenable staff into cantankerous, jibbering wrecks and driving highly esteemed customers up the wall with imbecilic requests to settle accounts several months after they have been paid. You will have heard all these things but still you are considering a computer for your business.

From the computer manufacturers' expensive and often glossy advertising in the press and on television, you will have heard the claims about the advance of computer technology. Certainly the advances have been impressive. If motor cars had advanced in technology and price at the same rate as computers, today you would be able to buy a roadster that on just one gallon of petrol could propel you, at well over the speed of sound, a distance of 1,000 miles. What is more, this nifty little runabout would cost you little more than a couple of hundred pounds.

The trouble is, to take the analogy a little further, many people have no need or indeed desire to drive around like that. It is the same with computers. Who wants to be saddled with a complex technological miracle when what you really want is the computer equivalent of a nippy runabout? For this reason it is vital, from the outset of your foray into the computer world, to identify what you need from a computer, rather than what the manufacturer wants to sell you.

You will no doubt have friends with computers in the business world. 'Couldn't do without it, old boy! 'Course it rules my life now; when it goes down we're totally stuck!' Despite this reliance on a machine that can cause untold disruption in a business, people continue to use computers, and more and more are introducing them for the first time. No matter what your friends and business acquaintances may say they keep their computers because, measured overall, their machines are still considered 'a good thing'.

It is true that some businesses try computerisation, find it does not measure up to their expectations and get out of it again. Indeed, a recent survey of over 500 businesses, large and small, discovered that around only 50 per cent believed the installation of computers had been a success. The trend is improving and it seems that fewer businesses are experiencing quite so many difficulties. Certainly many more are turning to computers than are getting out of them. Once a company installs a computer they tend to stick with it. Often there is a painful learning process because the whole process of introducing computers was not thought through. You, though, will not fall into that trap because in the next couple of chapters we shall attempt to learn from the mistakes of others by fully considering your computer needs.

The accounting miracle

Most business people first turn their thoughts to computers when they consider the welter of time-consuming, repetitive work associated with the accounts that are the backbone of any well run firm. Invoices, statements, ledgers, VAT, wages and PAYE are at best tedious, at worst tedious *and* unproductive.

Computers work best when they are asked to perform tedious, repetitive and boring tasks! So let us immediately bring in a computer and sort out the accounts. Yes... but there is still much more to be considered. Are you really going to consign your accounts to a machine?

There is now available a fair choice of computers and, more important, programs which will enable you eventually to run all your normal accountancy operations by machine. I stress the word eventually because, although the computer and its software (explained on page 32) will indeed be able to perform all manner of accountancy tasks, it is quite a different matter to get it to fit in with your way of working and thinking. In the end there will be a period of mutual sparring between your company and the computer until you arrive at a working compromise which both understand.

Stock control

Another area you might like to consider is stock control. If you are a manufacturer, a computer can help you keep track of raw materials (goods inwards or inputs) and finished goods (goods outwards or outputs). It can also link with your sales ledger to monitor stock levels of finished goods and give early warnings when you are about to run out of your award winning, top selling line. You can even get the computer to raise requisitions for raw materials to meet new production demands. (The ultimate will come when your computer talks directly through a telephone link to your supplier's computer, and between them they work out your needs while you and your supplier spend a gentle afternoon on the golf course.) Be warned, though, that such complex computer functions require highly sophisticated software to make things happen in the way you want. The more sophisticated the software, the longer it will take to integrate into your way of working, and it is your way of working, not the computer manufacturer's, that counts in the long run!

Plan to meet your financial fate

The reason most businesses install a computer is to provide an easy and streamlined means of financial accounting. Sales can be recorded, invoices produced, statements compiled. Management can keep track of the current state of payments from customers in relation to goods despatched. Regular printouts of aged debtors can be had. All this helps a vigilant business manager to guard against strain on the company's cash flow.

A computer can help you keep track of your bills and take full advantage of credit terms by reminding you when it is time to pay.

Many people would argue that before the advent of the business microcomputer, small businesses had hardly heard of financial planning, apart from the plan submitted to the bank to support a loan application. If it happened at all it was done by the accountant. Now there is no excuse, because every business computer makes great claims for the range of financial planning packages that can be run with the greatest of ease. On closer examination it is perhaps a little difficult to understand what all the fuss is about.

Financial planning programs will be mainly used by just you and a handful of staff. Its importance as a management tool is for individuals to assess. One drawback is that sitting in front of a computer playing with imaginary figures takes time, the one thing most business people are short of (apart from cash to develop the business). Time spent closeted with the computer is time that might be better spent elsewhere. On the shop floor, perhaps, geeing up morale; on the phone, bringing in new business; out and about making new contacts. Even if you don't neglect those areas of the business, the people who will really pay the price for time lost to the computer could well be your family.

Spreadsheets

One aspect of financial planning revolves around the setting up of what is known as a spreadsheet — a series of columns into which figures are inserted to correspond to income and expenditure on, usually, a month-by-month basis. The secret (the computer manufacturers would say beauty) of doing it on computer is that you can quite literally play about with the figures. When just one figure is changed the rest of the figures in the spreadsheet are automatically amended by the computer to correspond with the different input. This enables you to play 'What if?' games with your business. The possibilities can be quite amusing, if somewhat in the realms of fantasy: 'What if I up my turnover by 200 per cent and double my margins?'

Having said that, the use of a financial planning spreadsheet can have distinct advantages. No company can really afford to be without some idea about where they are trying to take the business. Spreadsheets can be used to set up financial targets both for profit and loss and cash flow. As the real figures come in they can be inserted against those in the budget. Month by month you, as manager of your business, can get an accurate assessment of how you are performing against any given targets. Bank managers can often be impressed by this, assuming the figures are going the right way!

A wonderful way with words

There is no doubt that, apart from its ability to handle figures at high speeds, the other main area where a computer can help a business is in the field of word processing. It is possible, using the simplest word processing programs, to produce high quality finished text to a consistently high standard, usually better than ordinary typewriting methods could ever have achieved. But to consider word processing as merely a substitute for the typewriter is grossly to undervalue its potential for developing any business.

In essence, word processing offers you the facility to create tracts of words, edit them, shape the text, store and retrieve it at will, at speeds much greater than with conventional methods. Now all of that does sound as if it has come straight from a manufacturer's glossy brochure, but I am convinced that word processing can be a real boon to many businesses. The only limitation on its potential is the imagination of the people involved in using it.

So how can a company make good use of word processing? For a start it can help with all those standard letters: reminders about overdue payments; advice-of-receipt notes; covering letters for price-lists, catalogues etc.

'But we can have standard letters printed,' I hear you say. That is true, but they still look like standard letters. They have to be filled in by hand and when they are, they usually look messy. How do you react when you receive a standard letter? Isn't it that much easier to ignore? With word processing even a standard letter can be made to look exclusive to the person on the receiving end. And this is the secret of word processing. Used correctly it can greatly enhance a company's image and bring it closer to its customers: every printed company communication can be personal.

There are those who think word processing can eliminate the typing pool and others who think that typing pools should have been eliminated years ago on the grounds of sheer humanity, but that is another issue. In any event *it is unlikely that the introduction of word processing will result in any significant reduction in staff.*

That said we perhaps ought to consider that the introduction of word processing will mean greater efficiency and, above all, better presentation of company documents. It will also mean that once trained, staff should have extra time to spend on more directly productive work. Approached in the right way, the introduction of word processing will make it easier for certain members of staff to offer much more to the company than when

15

they were tied up with typewriters for much of their day.

That is not to say that the introduction of word processing means you can throw the typewriter out of the window. One firm did just that and the managing director (himself a keen computer buff) had a near riot on his hands when the word processing program crashed for the umpteenth time and staff could not get their work done. Word processing must be introduced slowly and looked upon as an addition to rather than a replacement for existing methods.

So what else does it do? Well, it allows the management team to try for themselves various corporate messages. Brochure copy can be called up on a video screen and various versions edited from one original text. In businesses where the same form of words is used over and over again this facility can create real savings in time. Solicitors, for example, are always drawing up leases, wills, contracts, divorces and so on. By having these 'precedents' stored on magnetic disc the solicitor has merely to fill in the relevant names and addresses to create a new document. Only when that document has been finally approved (and it can be presented electronically in any number of drafts) will it be printed out in its definitive form.

Even greater efficiency could be achieved if firms using word processing were prepared to change some of their working practices. This will be discussed more fully in the next chapter. Many companies with word processors are not getting the best value from them because of what can only be described as keyboard phobia, often based on pure snobbery. For years the typewriter keyboard has been seen as a symbol of office tyranny: 'typing is women's work, women are subservient creatures'.

The computer manufacturers have long recognised keyboard phobia (the irrational fear of keyboards). Some have introduced all manner of devices to ensure that the male executive who is, of course, cut out for much better things, does not have to soil his hands by typing. However, when it comes to word processing there is for the time being no alternative (until, that is, voice-actuated computers and complementary software carve a real foothold in the market). Typing is certainly a skill and it takes time to learn how to do it well. But with word processing the typing process is easier, eradicating errors simpler.

There is no doubt that for word processing to be really effective more people in the company should learn to type (and therefore know how to use the processor) and that group of people should include *all* management!

File it

What do you do with all the junk mail that bounces through the door every day? Probably most of it gets thrown away, and anything that might be useful is filed. But we all know that filing is a tedious job and what is more, finding a piece of information can often be more tedious still. Not only that, filing takes up valuable office space — no one likes to see an office totally cluttered up with a welter of filing cabinets brimming over with paper, but a computer can help you store much more information, in a much smaller space. It can also enable you to find a relevant piece of information far more efficiently than any physical filing system, no matter how well cross-indexed that system might be.

The computer people call such a system a database, but it is best thought of as a very large filing cabinet. You could, for example, have every one of your customers listed in your database, together with their credit status, the amount of money they spend, details of the last transaction; even their spouse's name (useful in the preliminaries when you have to ring them to chase up a payment). The database will help you sort through your records and compile lists based on any criteria you like to establish; how many in one particular part of the country (or even the world); those who spent more than a certain amount in the last 12 months; by product groups. Then, usually in conjunction with a suitable word processing program, you can get the computer to write personalised letters to them, and print out sticky labels to speed the addressing of envelopes. The possibilities are indeed, as the glossy advertising says, endless!

Work expands to meet capacity

There is a kind of Parkinson's Law that seems to operate with computers: the amount of work you thought needed computerising in your business tends to expand to fill the capabilities of the computer you buy. There is another law which dictates that no matter how carefully you choose your computer system it never quite matches up to your original expectations, or if it does, you rapidly discover that your business has outstripped the capacity of the machine, but this eventuality is the kind of happy development most businesses would relish.

This chapter will ensure that you 'get your head straight' about why you think you really need a computer. You may have been led to consider other aspects of your business which might benefit from some kind of computer input, but remember here that the key word is benefit. It might be nice to have a spot of word processing in addition to the originally defined need for, say, a computerised accounts operation, but can you really afford to dabble in any part of your business? As we shall discover later, introducing computers is not for the faint-hearted; you have to plan for it and be prepared to follow the plan through, but above all you must know what you need.

Checklist

So a checklist for a specification which will describe all the business systems and procedures you are expecting the computer to cover. I need a computer for:

1. *Financial accounting*
   Sales order processing
   Despatch and invoicing
   Statement production
   (If accounts are the main use for the computer, have you discussed it with your accountant?)
2. *Financial planning* (for the start-up of a new business or expansion; to help define the effects of investing in, for example, marketing a specific service or product)
3. *Production/stock control*
   Purchasing
   Stock control
4. *Word processing*
5. *Database filing*
   Creating mailing lists
   Cross referencing suppliers
6. *I'm now frightened. I don't need a computer!*

Case study: Overcoming fears

Martin Deeley is manager of the Business Information Technology Centre at the Dorset Institute of High Technology. He has direct experience of the importance of training, particularly when it comes to improving the performance of people with existing, computer-related skills.

Why Do You Want a Computer?

We've been involved with the installation of computers in a public authority. When we went in we discovered that computers still held a fear in many minds; a 'mystique' which has to be removed. The change from manual to electric and then to electronic typewriters has been a gradual, easy one. However, the change from manual to computerised accounting, filing or even word processing we found to be too large a step for many who simply were not prepared for the computer revolution. Among the fears expressed by many people were, 'We shall lose data' or, 'Files will get corrupted' or even, 'We are frightened of "breaking" the machine.' On further analysis we discovered that much of this was caused quite simply by lack of basic knowledge of modern computers and a very limited understanding of the simple controls and 'housekeeping' procedures now widely used in the computer world.

Staff with keyboard experience, initially at least, showed more confidence in the operation of a micro computer simply because of their familiarity with this form of information entry. There is no doubt in my mind that widespread training in simple keyboard skills helped overcome many initial fears about actually touching a computer and receiving error messages or the occasional attention-getting 'Beep'!

With the public authority, which was trying to introduce a computerised recording system, we helped to organise a keyboard skills course for all staff involved, with the result that the entry of data is quicker and more accurate. Not only that, much of the concern about operating the terminal has now been removed. Some members of staff were reluctant to take the course and on investigation we discovered a number of causes. Some considered the course below them; others were concerned they would not be able to reach the required standard; others were simply being plain bloody minded and reacting against management and change. In all events we found that the best course of action was to make sure that at all times the trainer remained supportive and encouraging. It is vital to motivate each individual to achieve a level at which they can perform with a degree of pride. *Loss of face must be avoided at all costs*, particularly when training is carried out within a group of colleagues.

It is most important not to underestimate the 'shame factor'. Initially there was a reluctance for managers and employees to admit that they knew little about computers, managers claiming that they only required information from a machine which was operated by a member of staff and therefore there was no need to know about the machine and its software capabilities. As we were gradually able to explain the potential of the machine, attitudes changed and demand for a computer appreciation course specifically aimed at managers rapidly increased. Mixed management and staff courses are also proving invaluable, primarily because they increase understanding about other people's jobs.

Chapter 2

Who Will Use the Computer?

A simple question; there ought to be a simple, quite obvious answer. The computer will be used by... well by...? Yes, not so obvious is it? Certainly all staff should be able to read computer printouts and thankfully they are getting easier to read as computers become more 'user friendly'. But let us turn our attention to the day-to-day use of the computer itself.

For a computer to operate effectively, information needs to be accurate and fed in in the right way — the way the computer likes it. Computers thrive on special diets of information. Give them the wrong thing or even the right thing in the wrong way and they reject it. 'Rubbish in, rubbish out' is the well worn phrase. If the wrong information is fed into the computer you cannot expect the machine to process it and come up with the right answer. The really smart computer is still a long way off for the average business user. Remember, computers are really best at doing boring jobs; you cannot expect them to be other than non-thinking automatons. Therefore, the key person is the one who links your business with the computer. In time he or she could well become the key person (apart from yourself, of course) for the business as a whole. If you have any doubts on that score just consider what this individual will be responsible for.

To this one person you will have entrusted the safe keeping of all your accounts, all your word processing, all your filing and so on, everything that makes your business tick. Just think of the potential power all in the hands of one person. The person who is at the 'interface' between the computer and your business.

'But one person cannot possibly do all that,' I hear you say. Of course not, more people will have to be involved. But that brings us back to the original question — who?

In the main computers still depend very much on information being fed into them by means of a keyboard. This simple fact has led to a perhaps understandable trend among employers to throw the operation of the new computer to those who by office tradition know most about keyboards and we have seen the upgrading of typists and secretaries to 'operate the computer'. No doubt many such upgradings work. The people involved, after perhaps an initial Luddite approach to the advent of some new-fangled monster, usually take to the computer and become proficient. However, to consign any computer installation to a minority of people is to overlook areas of tremendous potential.

Power to the people?

We have already mentioned the potential power wielded by those who know the ins and outs of the business computer; and such power concentrated in a very few hands can be very dangerous for a business. There have been numerous examples of industrial action being strategically limited to the computer department of a large organisation which, although involving only a fraction of the company's employees, has had the same effect as a mass walk-out by the entire work-force. Even governments are not immune. All this is very frightening for the businessman contemplating the installation of a computer.

The good news is that while large concerns need to have specialised departments to operate their computers, smaller businesses can spread the expertise. There are dividends in terms of peace of mind by following this policy, but there are also very real positive benefits. Which brings us back to the initial question, 'Who will use the computer?'

Computers in business should be capable of operation by as many people within the firm as possible.

'But isn't that all a great waste of time?' I hear you ask. No it is not.

First, by spreading the involvement in the new technology as broadly as possible you will reduce the 'them and us' factor that accompanies any innovation.

Second, by ensuring that people are involved right from the outset, difficulties in making the computer relate to an individual business can be ironed out almost before they occur. There is nothing worse than a computer program being designed at great expense with due consultation between the programmers and senior members of the company only to find that lower levels in the firm do not operate as they used to in the days when the management were themselves on the shop-floor! Discovering that fact too late in the day can be very painful.

The third advantage to spreading computer literacy within the company is an obvious one. The more people you have who can use the computer the less likely you are to be held to ransom in industrial relations terms by a small but vital computer elite. This is one of the few areas where smaller businesses can score over large operations. It is an advantage which should be grasped with both hands.

How much knowledge?

It is perhaps as well at this stage to set a limit on just how computer literate people need to be in business. Do they, for example, need to learn computer languages in order to give instructions to the computer? The short answer to that is no. True, some business people learn one of the simpler languages such as BASIC (often as a result of trying to keep up with their children on a home computer) but although it is possible to use that knowledge to alter or even create programs for business use, unless you are really keen, it is best left alone. The ready-made programs are already in computer language. Computer programming is time-consuming and not many business people would have the time to commit to it. In business, computer languages are the preserve of the expert who has to use the language to create the results you want. If you start trading jargon with him or her you will come off worst.

You may feel, though, that it would be useful for some of your employees to acquire computer literacy, including programming languages. BASIC is one of the simpler languages but not all business-related software is written in BASIC, and even where BASIC is the programming language, some software uses adaptations of the language. If you are planning to have staff alter, adapt or create programs, it is as well to check that their expertise matches the programming language.

Other languages, PASCAL, COBOL, FORTRAN for example, are generally used for more advanced applications — complicated financial packages and scientific calculations. If you need that kind of computing power you will probably employ dedicated (expensive) experts with a thorough working knowledge of these languages.

In short, don't worry about computer languages, just concern yourself with ensuring you and your staff understand what the computer can do for the business, not how it does it.

How many people should be involved?

Obviously the number of people involved in the computer installation project will vary from one business to another and may depend on factors such as the time available. Can you afford to divert people away from otherwise productive employment? More of this in the next chapter.

The first stage is to draw up two lists. First, a list of people for whom you believe ability to use the computer is essential. This list will depend on what use you are going to make of your computer. If it is for accounts, then the people who operate your present manual ledger system will need to be involved. Word processing will require secretarial staff, and so on.

This first list will essentially be a minimum number of people you can get away with. I say get away with to stress that in reality it is your second list — of people who might reasonably benefit (and therefore benefit the company) — which you may find in time provides even greater potential for the computer than you had originally envisaged.

On the second list could be, for example, sales people. If they know how the computer handles customers' accounts they will be in a better position to service your clients (and incidentally, but perhaps even more importantly, chase up overdue accounts). Systems are already available whereby sales people can carry their own computer terminal in a briefcase linked by telephone or even radio to the company's main computer. Through such a terminal the salesman can check the availability of stock, initiate an order, get an update of the customers' current credit status and so on. You might not have that quite in mind yet for your business but there are obvious advantages in having salesmen who know something about the computer age.

You might like to consider including certain grades of people involved directly in production. If the computer is to be used for stock control it would be an advantage for them to know how stock and raw material levels are set and monitored by the computer, rather than simply work from an impersonal computer printout. It would also give them a clearer idea of the relationship between input/output and wastage/shrinkage!

If you have drawn up your lists correctly you may find that over 50 per cent of your work-force will appear on one or other of your lists. Ideally you should expect to amalgamate the lists to produce the maximum number of people for whom computer literacy will either be essential or at least beneficial to the company. Educating over half of the company's employees may not be exactly what you had in mind when you had that first twinkle in the eye to computerise the accounts, but make no mistake, failure to involve a sizeable number of the work-force in the installation and operation of a computer can lead to trouble later on.

The introduction of computer literacy need not be a completely daunting prospect. Once you have drawn up your two lists you can then rearrange the names on each in order of priority, that is who needs to acquire computer literacy first. Obviously those on list one, the essential users, will get first bite of the computer cherry. You can then work through the second list and assess the order in which you would like to train the computer 'beneficial' personnel. Having done that you can also apply a desirable time-scale. Desirable rather than actual because, as we shall discuss later, the realities of training are usually a far cry from what is 'desirable'. For the moment you should simply work out a timetable that would, in an ideal world, be right for the business. It is not necessary to rush through the training process, but unless you set a timetable the chances are it will never get done.

Consultation cures criticism

One area where it is absolutely essential to involve everyone as early as possible is that of consultation. Introducing a computer, however small, will bring about such a radical change in working practice that lack of consultation with a broad spectrum of the work-force will lead eventually to disaster.

Computer disasters occur essentially on two levels. One, you get the wrong computer system because, to your amazement, you did not know as much about existing working practices as you thought you did. Staff who will be using the computer on a daily basis should be offered a big say in what *they* see as priorities for a computer. They will know exactly what they want it to do; they will know how much better it will have to be to justify all the time and trouble, not to mention money, that have gone into installing it in the first place. They will be using it on a day-to-day basis and will soon be able to spot, once the machine is up and running, whether it is performing satisfactorily. Not only that, experience shows that they are likely to be much tougher (to the point of seeming unreasonable) in dealings with the suppliers of the computer hardware, software or, indeed, consultancy. After all, their jobs will directly depend on it.

The computer represents a major revolution in working practice; it brings with it major fears. Among those fears is the thought that it might result in lost jobs; it might downgrade the quality of a job; it might upgrade a job, making it impossible for existing staff to compete; it might damage the health of an operator. There are other objections which could be raised at the prospect of introducing computer technology. To anyone with half a knowledge of computers most of the objections will appear trivial in the extreme. However, in the mind of the employee the threat of a computer can loom very large. It is essential not to underestimate the vehemence of reaction to a computer system installed from 'on high'.

In some companies the introduction of the computer will be seized upon by the trades unions as a very useful bargaining opportunity. The unions, perhaps understandably, want to get the best deal for their members. If the management wants to bring in computers, they argue, necessitating a whole new set of skills to be learnt by the work-force, then someone will have to pay. And we all know who that someone will be! It is not unreasonable to pay more for extra work and the learning of different skills. After all, management will, presumably have evaluated the increase in efficiency the computer will bring about. Is it not fair and just for the work-force to share in the proceeds of that increased efficiency?

If at this stage you are starting to get edgy once again, be assured that such feelings are totally justified. If you are not feeling decidedly jumpy, the chances are you are deluding yourself about either the level of difficulty you may encounter or your capability to deal with it painlessly. New technology agreements are fertile ground for trades union negotiators.

By now you will be convinced, I hope, of one of two things. Either you will have given up all hope of ever bringing in a computer, or you will believe root and branch in the absolute necessity for consultation. Consultation means detailed discussions, at length and in depth. But who do you talk to? If the trades unions are going to cause so much trouble, perhaps they should be the first point of contact. There are strong arguments in favour of such a plan, but in my view the unions can generally serve only to illuminate part of the computer debate. Principally jobs and money. Certainly involve the union if there is one in your company, but for something as significant as the introduction of a computer, you should be aiming for a broader based consultative process.

Talking takes time

Proper consultation really does take up a lot of time. Most entrepreneurial business people like to feel that once they have taken a decision the policy should be implemented as quickly as possible. Certainly this is an attitude favoured by the more thrusting employers.

We can all cite cases where delay for consultation would have negated the very reason for the change in policy in the first place. John Egan, the man who quite remarkably turned round the fortunes of Jaguar cars, bringing about a spectacularly oversubscribed flotation on the stock market, was once asked about his approach to consultation. He needed to introduce far-reaching reforms in working practice to stem the flow of haemorrhaging cash. It was put to him that perhaps he did not spend as much time as was prudent consulting the work-force about the changes. His reply? 'You don't expect the pilot of an aircraft to go back and ask the passengers how to get it out of its current nosedive!' Strong words, echoed no doubt by many an entrepreneur.

However, we will assume that your business is not in a nosedive. If it is, what are you doing even contemplating a computer? The computer will not help you turn your business around, and in any event, if you are in dire straits you could not possibly afford the time needed to bring in a computer operation successfully.

We shall work on the basis that the business is ticking over nicely and that (having read Chapter 1) you have defined the need for a computer to enhance an already well organised set of business systems. The first rule of consultation is *start early*. Most business people will first take the decision that they need a computer and then consult the staff over the way it is used. To avoid the pitfalls, there must be a long lead time between first discussions about the possible introduction of the computer and the machine coming through reception; a year would not be too long in some cases!

By now you will have defined your business needs, decided your priority areas for computerisation and worked out your two lists of 'essential' and 'beneficial' users together with their priorities. It really is time to talk, but it is at this point that you can make two fatal mistakes:

1. Delegate the installation of the computer system to a subordinate in your management structure.
2. Set up a special 'computer working party'.

On the face of it, both courses of action sound quite reasonable, but let us take a closer look at what is being proposed.

Point one: you as an entrepreneurial business person have developed a grasp of the imperative for introducing a computer, but you know the arguments only from one point of view, yours! Here you are about to get your most valuable input and then you hand over the project to someone lower down the company ladder. Surely this is the one time when it is essential to keep 'hands on'? There is only one possible management reason for handing over now: if something goes wrong you (and the workforce) will have somebody else to blame. That really is not a justifiable state of affairs.

Another factor is that you, having presumably taken the initial decision to look seriously at introducing computers will, as boss, be the only person capable of maintaining the management clout essential if the project is to be carried through as swiftly as possible, even if the result is that you abandon the attempt.

Let us look at the second point. Surely a working party of interested employees will be best equipped to analyse what the world of computers has on offer and how it can fit in with existing working practices? Of course. Not only that, you may be able to attract one or two employees who know a bit about computers, either from previous jobs or because they play about with a Sinclair Spectrum at home. Indeed, they would probably be delighted to sit on the working party. But pause to think. The last people you want on the working party are those who may be predisposed towards computers, or have prejudices against them. Computers in themselves, or people's knowledge of them, do not matter. What really counts is the vital question, can computers work for this particular business?

What you really need to get to the bottom of that fundamental point is a group of enlightened sceptics. Enlightened about the way your business works and ways in which it could be better; sceptical about computers, computer people and their jargon. Such people should not be hard to find within the firm and they should be encouraged to become involved in the consultation process. Any consultation should be spread across the company.

Every department affected by the proposed computerisation should be represented; you may feel that others too should have a voice.

A consultation process based on the principle of quality circles lends itself well. Each department nominates/elects from the employees a representative to come along to the consultation meetings. He or she then reports back verbally to colleagues and this verbal report is backed up by official written minutes of the meeting which are given wide circulation within the company. Depending on the lead time available for the consultation process, meetings can be monthly, fortnightly or even daily.

Access to the quality circle should not necessarily be restricted to nominated representatives. It should be possible, production demands allowing, for anyone with something to say to have access to the circle. Circles can expand, contract or even subdivide as deemed necessary. What is important is accurate and comprehensive minuting of its proceedings. This not only keeps people outside the circle informed, but also provides the basis for a dynamic approach to the consultation process, whereby real progress is maintained and the circle does not come to be regarded as a talking shop. A bad circle is one where all the discussion is in circles!

Throughout the consultation process it will fall to you to maintain the impetus, which brings us to perhaps the most important point. If you thought computerisation was something which you would not have to dirty your hands with, think again. The first person on your list of essential users should be you. The boss should *never* delegate his own computer literacy! It is a daunting prospect. Learning to use computers entails an element of 'back to school', but if you do not show the way, how can you expect anyone else to?

Summary

1. Identify essential computer users.
2. Assess those who might benefit from computer literacy.
3. Consult, and do it early.
4. Be prepared to offer a high level of personal commitment.

Still keen on introducing a computer? Good. Now comes the really interesting bit. How are you going to pay for it?

Case study: Training

The impact of computerisation on a business cannot be overstressed. However, computers usually offer a chance for everyone, given the opportunity of sufficient training, to shine, as Martin Deeley, Manager of the Business Information Technology Centre at the Dorset Institute of High Technology explains:

> When we installed computers in one company it was interesting to note that during an introduction to computing using 'hands on' experience, the typists and clerical assistants initially seemed far more confident and actually ribbed the managers in their attempts to key in information. However, when spreadsheets and programming were attempted, the roles changed and the managers were able to use their skills and experience to the full.

Martin Deeley has another example of how training costs can be trimmed:

> We've designed computer literacy courses for two large international organisations. These are available to any member of staff; half of the training is in works time, the other half in their own time. One of the companies offers the additional motivation that if an employee completes the course to the satisfaction of the trainers and the company, he or she will be given a home micro computer!

How's that for an incentive? Would it work for your company? However you look at it training is expensive, but as Martin Deeley puts it:

> There is no doubt that effective training can minimise many of the problems associated with the introduction of a computer system. To be effective, training should be carried out by a professional body with experience and understanding of what is required to achieve the organisation's objectives. Money spent on training is a long-term investment and should be viewed in that context.

Chapter 3

Can You Really Afford a Computer?

This is by far the most important chapter in the book. In the unlikely event that before reading the first two chapters you thought computerisation was a quick, efficient, and above all, inexpensive method of bringing extra effectiveness to your business, you will by now be thinking somewhat differently! At one stage you may have been seduced by the lure of newspaper advertisements assuring you that computers have never been cheaper. You may also have got as far as assessing the price you might have to pay for a computer.

On the face of it computers are inexpensive and what is more they are getting cheaper by the day. Surely your business can easily afford the cost? I have no doubt that it can, but only as far as you can really quantify what the real costs are. Possibly you have so far taken into account only the prices quoted for the hardware, and perhaps a little bit of software.

Hardware

Hardware is the name given to all the 'hard' bits of the computer system: the processor unit, the keyboard, the screen, the printer and so on — the bits you can actually reach out and touch.

When people first start to discuss computers, it tends to be the hardware that gets mentioned most:

'I've just taken delivery of an Apple.'

'My kids are really into their Commodore 64.'

'You should see how the "mouse" works on the Mackintosh!'

This trend towards centring all discussion on the hardware is perhaps understandable. After all, the hardware is there for everyone to see. Not only that, the history of the computer business shows that it's the big companies with substantial tooling and production back-up which cut the mustard when

So You Think Your Business Needs a Computer?

it comes to churning out thousands of computers a week. Little wonder then that the production effort carries such powerful marketing strategies.

One computer manufacturer discovered through its market research that there was considerable sales resistance among middle and senior managers to one of its models, which had been selling well in applications where it was to be used primarily by women working at lower levels in the company structure. However, further research uncovered the fact that it was not status which was the major factor, but colour! After consultation with its design department, the company changed the colour of the screen, processor and keyboard casings from soft, feminine fawn/beige to tough, macho steel grey/black. Suddenly every executive wanted one!

In spite of what the advertisements say, in business it is software that really counts, time and time again.

Software

Software is the name given to the set of instructions fed into the hardware that tells it how to do the tasks required.

To get a better grasp of the differences between hardware and software we need look no further than the human brain itself. The mass of tissue that makes up the grey matter can be regarded as the hardware (with the skull acting as the protective outer casing); what we actually *think* via tiny electrical impulses is the software. When someone dies, the brain (hardware) remains intact, but the individual (presumably!) ceases to think — the software is no more. The same happens when you switch off a computer. The big difference is you can reactivate a computer by switching it back on, and by feeding in more software get it 'thinking' once again.

It may seem that we have digressed somewhat from the business of computing costs, but it is important to grasp what is at the root of all decision making on the introduction of business computers. *Without software, hardware is useless. Software determines the overall effectiveness of a computer system.*

Of course that is an oversimplification; naturally the hardware has to be capable of coping with all that a software program demands, but that is relatively easy to arrange. Finding the right software in the first place is not so easy.

In Chapter 1 we stressed how vital it is for the computer system to operate so as to fit in with your existing business systems; too often in the past the reality has been quite the reverse. A certain amount of compromise is usually necessary, and this is usually dependent on how logical your existing business systems are, of which more later, but the definition of a good software package revolves around how well it fits in with your particular way of working.

It is not easy to produce one piece of catch-all software which is suitable for all business applications. This means the software developers have had to specialise, creating packages for much smaller markets. Some business applications require software to be written especially for them alone. Whether that applies to you will depend on how unique your business or its existing operating systems are. The chances are you will be able to use an existing package or indeed have an off-the-peg package modified to suit your needs.

What all this is leading up to is that you will have to pay for the privilege of having your computer hardware operate so as to cause your business as little upset as possible. While mass production in the hands of conglomerates such as IBM, Apple, Commodore, STC/ICL and so on has meant that hardware costs have been pared right back, software for the most part has followed a rather different route to the present day position. Software development is a much more diversified operation; at its lowest level it often amounts to little more than a one man cottage industry. Although cottage industries have always been regarded as being at the inexpensive end of the industrial spectrum, the real costs in producing software packages come from the sheer level of human input required. People who write software are usually intelligent and skilled; they don't normally sell themselves cheap!

So where does that leave us on the question of prices? While it is relatively easy for the business person to quantify what his hardware costs might be — anything from £2,000 to £100,000 — software costs can only be assessed on a 'how long is a piece of string?' basis. However, the average business wanting a range of basic computing ability from accounts, through word processing to database filing, can often reckon on the software costing another 50 per cent on top of the cost of the computer hardware itself, particularly if there is any special programming involved. So if you were planning to spend £3,000 or so on a basic business computer, start expecting to count the change out of £5,000! If you are looking for more sophisticated packages such as stock control, invoicing and so on, it could cost you much more.

Having said that, there are, with the increasing competition, more and more off-the-peg software packages which can be easily made to fit in with your business operation. Software prices are dropping too, but not as fast as those of the hardware.

The cost of thought

If you are approaching business computing in the right way you will be putting a lot of thought into the operation; several of your waking hours over many weeks will be taken up in consideration and analysis of the implications of computerisation. We have agreed that computerisation is too important a step not to be considered by you personally. You will also be involving your management colleagues and staff. Their time is money too. Try to quantify what all that means in terms of the business. It's not sufficient to look at just the hourly rate aspect of time spent on discussing and thinking about computers; you also have to assess the effect on the business of that time not being spent on directly productive work.

In Chapter 2 we discussed the implications of allowing enough time to analyse and assess the impact of computerisation. Lead times of up to a year were mentioned, allowing for consultation and consideration by management and staff alike. Let us now try to quantify that time. There are two stages of development you might like to consider for your staff:

1. Attaining a general level of computer literacy within the firm.
2. Achieving sufficient skill in computers and understanding of systems to enable a computer system to operate within the business.

Most employers skip the first level and go straight to the second, arguing, 'Why should I teach people about general computing principles in the firm's time?' Most business people would certainly have some sympathy with that argument; after all, businesses exist to make profits, not indulge in some kind of technological philanthropy! However, the achievement of level two is much easier if staff have already been through level one. Not only that, it is possible to reap rewards from the fact that learning about computing on a general rather than specifically business-related level benefits the member of staff as an individual. Consider the case study in Chapter 2 of the company which offered a micro computer as an incentive to any member of staff who successfully completed a computing course; it proved to be such a useful carrot to counter the stick that only half the course was carried out in works' time.

It is, of course, for individual company principals to decide what the firm can afford in time, both in terms of consultation and training. But as Martin Deeley pointed out, 'Computer training must be viewed as a long-term investment'. It is as important to invest in the skills of your staff as it is in the computer hardware and software itself.

You may now be thinking, 'This talk of training is all very well, but surely I can get away with just the bare minimum?' You may well be right, but remember, you will indeed be 'getting away with it'. The importance of getting the staff on your side (not to mention the side of the computer) cannot be stressed too much. Supposing you install your system with the bare minimum of training. It's all working wonderfully. The staff are just getting used to it and believing that their couple of days' on-site training is all paying off. Suddenly the computer for no apparent reason goes haywire and begins to look very poorly indeed. Morale can quickly go out of the window. The longer the computer stays 'down' the more likely are staff to reach for their ledgers and quill pens once again. If that happens it'll take a whole new process of persuasion to restore their confidence in computers. The longer the training period, the more likely they are to stick with it in the face of adversity. Not only that, they may well be far better placed to help solve any snags or bugs which may arise (and there will be plenty).

However much of your time, and that of your staff, you decide to invest in the computer, do try to make some kind of accurate analysis in terms of hours spent over a period. It may not be a bad idea then to work out the cost on an hourly rate basis, where that is applicable, but you would be wise to consider that the hourly rate formula does not take fully into account the real costs. Training and consultation are, in the short term at least, non-productive in terms of bringing new revenue to the company. You should make allowance for potential revenue lost. As a rule of thumb, try doubling the hourly rate!

Looking at the previous couple of doom-laden paragraphs, you may well be asking yourself why anyone goes in for computerisation at all. Reaping the benefits must be viewed as a long-term expectation, but the costs are real and they generally have to be paid for up-front. In fact, *it is unlikely that many firms will see any real financial benefits from the introduction of computers for at least two years!*

There — that is something they don't tell you in the computer ads.

Matching systems and software

Computer people just love to talk about 'systems'. Their very hierarchy enshrines the word. Every computer programmer longs for the day when he or she can become a systems analyst. It's a very grand name for a pretty mundane, if logical job. In the early days of computers the systems analyst was the person who worked out ways in which a computer could do the range of complicated tasks required.

Traditionally, systems analysts would spend several weeks, or even months, touring a company, clipboard in hand getting a feel for the business. They would then spend much time breaking down the complex functions of the operation into a series of much simpler tasks capable of being handled by the computer. In the good old days analysts might uncover all manner of illogical or unsound practices in the course of their investigations, but it was relatively unusual for any great changes to be made. After all, was not the whole purpose of the computerisation to improve the efficiency of existing staff and working operations? When you bought a computer, you tended to buy it as a package with the software, and because of the absence of off-the-peg software, fitting the computer around the business was a much easier task. Psychologically, too, there was less inclination for the champions of a new and growing industry to start telling older and wiser businessmen that their systems were wrong. If they wanted a computer to improve their existing business, then indeed that was the computer they were going to get. After all, he who pays the piper...

Today it's not quite like that: hardware and software tend to get sold separately, like washing machines and soap powder. True, hardware manufacturers may well recommend certain software packages, but that does not get the average business user much further; look at the range of soap powders recommended by just one big washing machine manufacturer! The chances are that the average business will have to use one of the existing software packages or have one modified to suit its particular operation. Either choice is better than the alternative of having software especially written for you — the likelihood is you simply won't be able to afford it. What that means is that you will have to be better disposed towards adapting your business to the software, rather than the other way around.

That does not necessarily mean a vast upheaval in working practices. What it does mean is that, possibly for the first time ever, you will have to analyse exactly how your business operates. For many that could well prove a salutary experience! Take, for example, the entrepreneur who has built his business up from scratch; he, it can be safely assumed, never sat down at the outset and drew up a set of operating systems; it all just evolved.

Let's look at what happens when he gets an order in for 10 gallons of his award winning ice cream. We'll assume the order comes by phone and is written down by whoever answers the phone in the office. While the customer is hanging on, that person shouts down into the yard where Jack, the factory manager is busy ticking off one of the drivers for being late.

'How soon can we let Mr So-and-So have 10 gallons of ice cream?'

'What flavour?'

'Vanilla.'

'Vanilla? He'll be lucky, the last lot went out yesterday and we're not making till Thursday!'

All this is relayed to the customer who then asks for an alternative flavour, and the process starts once again. Not terribly efficient is it? It has to be admitted that it is also a bit of an exaggeration. I mean, what manufacturing and sales operation would last long with that kind of approach? But just think of the number of times you've been after something from a supplier and a shout to the factory floor, or a phone call to Bert in stores has followed a quite ordinary enquiry for a quite ordinary product line.

Now a computer person will tell you that computers can help

you avoid all that, but if he does he is only telling you half the story. Let's look at the example again.

Someone rings up for 10 gallons of award winning ice cream. Wouldn't it be much better if sales calls came in on a specific telephone line with its own specific, easy-to-remember number? That way when that phone rings or flashes everyone knows it is a potential sale and the right person can answer the call. No need for a computer to organise that.

Let's also assume the right person to take an order is on hand and within arm's reach of the telephone. He or she might even let the phone ring long enough to grab the order pad especially designed with carbonless copies, colour coded for various departments: one for accounts; one for production; one for despatch; one as a packing note. He or she might even glance at the latest stock level figures, pinned up by the telephone and freshly updated that morning. Also pinned up are van delivery days, by area. The phone is answered, the order taken. The operator will note from the stock schedule that there's no 'award winning vanilla' and, if things are really efficient, there will be a note of the fact that they are planning to produce some more on Thursday. An alternative will be offered, again using the stock sheet. The customer accepts the alternative, is told which day he can expect delivery and the phone is put down. The order is then ready for processing. No computer needed so far! If things are running as they should be the various copies of the order will go out in the following priority:

1. *Despatch.* Let's get the customer his ice cream as soon as possible.
2. *Production.* Let's make sure we don't run out of this stock line.
3. *Accounts.* Let's get the money in.

Each department will get its copy order at about the same time, which doesn't really matter as long as delay in getting the order from the sales department is kept to a minimum. It's a one-site operation: messengers pick up paperwork at regular intervals; within a few hours everyone has a copy of the relevant paperwork. Our customer could well get his ice cream 'ere long. Still no need for a computer.

Of course there is no need for a computer, as long as you have plenty of staff of the right calibre available. On the face of it a computer handling that kind of operation would immediately be able to cut out the 'messenger' element of the work-force, but the possibility of cutting down such costs was recognised long before the advent of the microchip. Remember all those establishments that used vacuum tubes to ferry paperwork about? Some of them still do. As for the other categories of staff, it is unlikely that the computer will bring savings there. All that will happen is that, in theory at least, they will be able to perform their functions more efficiently. Introducing computers to that ice cream factory will have three main effects.

1. They will have to look at their operating systems. No more inefficient order taking/processing.
2. There will be a tangible cost of installing computerisation in terms of hardware and software.
3. Information about the sales/processing/despatch/production areas of the firm will be much more widely available.

Let's look at those points one by one. First, it can be no bad thing that a company is forced to look at its operating systems. Computerisation provides a good opportunity/excuse/justification for change and improvement.

Second, given sufficient lead time for analysis, consultation etc, it will be a relatively easy task to evaluate who needs access to the computer system. Clearly each department, sales, despatch, production, accounts, will need a computer terminal but most important, and this brings us to the third point, it is the extra terminals which will make the real difference. The managing director with his terminal can instantly assess the state of play with regard to any aspect of the business operation, at the touch of a few buttons.

How often does an MD's foray on to the shop floor become nothing more than a ritual?

'Morning Joe, how's it going?'

'OK, Boss, no problems at all.'

The MD accepts all this, no doubt with a pinch of salt, but unless he has a set of production figures supplied by his production director he'll not be in much of a position to argue with Joe's rose-tinted view of the world. Computers offer management the potential of knowing what they want to know, when they want to know it. If our award winning ice cream company had a marketing director he could, by tapping into the computer network via his own terminal, generate graphical displays of sales figures. Such displays could give him valuable insights into trends and help him plan a new marketing strategy based on knowledge gained from historical sales analysis.

So You Think Your Business Needs a Computer?

Similarly the production director could highlight bottlenecks which were slowing down output and gain a view not only of the overall efficiency of the production process, but also, by analysis of the breakdown frequency, decide which machinery should be replaced.

All this sounds very grand, and it would work, but only with a highly sophisticated integrated computer system. You will probably not be able to install such a system straight off and have it up and running overnight. Better to hasten slowly and install it section by section. This modular approach to computer installation will, when you do your initial costing, appear more expensive than an all-in, fully integrated package, but there are distinct advantages, of which more in Chapter 4. Back to costs!

Kennelling the computer

Finding somewhere for the computer to live is usually left till last, but it is a very real consideration; it can also be a costly one. Happily the days when computers had to be kept in purpose-built rooms, often with strengthened floors to take the weight of the valves on which their very operation depended are long gone.

Over the years computers have become much more resilient to the modern office environment, although they are still sensitive creatures. They do not, for example, like extremes of heat and cold. Humidity is a great enemy too. And if you spill a cup of coffee over one, well you can certainly bank on kissing a great deal of data goodbye, and possibly even the machine itself. Virtually all businesses will use floppy disks for data storage (explained in Chapter 6) and while computers themselves have become much hardier over the years, the disks are still very sensitive and open to corruption from magnetic fields, dust, human hairs and (here's the rub for many office users) even cigarette smoke. As for cigarette ash . . .! Perhaps you could use the computer as a good excuse for introducing a no smoking rule in the office.

Naturally computer terminals have to be placed where people can use them. This usually means on their desks, already cluttered, no doubt, by filing trays, telephones and the like. There are some in the computer business who still insist that computers will cut down on the amount of paper being pushed around an office. Those with a modicum of experience will claim no such thing.

We are still a long way from the paperless office for most businesses and the demand for 'hard' copy remains as strong as ever. Computers enable much more information to be processed and accessed. This results in more, not less paper in the office. Hard copies mean printers, printers take space and add more noise to an already noisy environment. It is true that printers can be shared between several screens, but only one screen can access the printer at a time so there is an obvious limit to the number of terminals that can link into one printer.

The temptation is to bank the printers together so that (given the correct software) many more terminals can be hooked up and use the first printer available. However, if you do bank two or more printers together you will probably have to find a separate room for them or invest in soundproof *acoustic hoods*. Without such investment two or more printers, chattering for most of the day, will try the patience (and the eardrums) of the most placid employee.

If desk space is at a premium you may find yourself being asked to invest in purpose-built computer desks. Some companies, particularly those where computers and instant communications are a must, have customised desks to suit their needs. However, there is plenty of off-the-peg computer furniture to be had, with accommodation for visual display unit, processor, and printer where necessary and still plenty of space for telephones, message trays and so on. Needless to say, though, a desk is only a desk; when it becomes a piece of computer furniture the price goes up. Yet another cost to be considered.

Computer stationery

We spoke of computers, by virtue of their capacity to process more information, having the potential to produce more paper. Experience shows that even in the best regulated businesses paper consumption goes up with the introduction of computers. For a start, particularly in the initial stages, paper is wasted as staff get to grips with the vagaries of the printers. Many printers which use continuous stationery (cheaper by far than single sheets which need a special feeder costing sometimes as much as the printer itself) automatically waste a sheet at either the beginning or end of a print run, sometimes both. This is an insignificant loss when you are printing reams of documents at once, but most businesses tend to use their printers intermittently for operations such as letter writing and so on; here the paper wastage can mount up.

And what about all that customised stationery you had printed last year at vast expense? Will it be suitable for your computer needs? You may have to decide to junk much of it. Of course, if you are allowing yourself enough lead time before introducing the computer system you may have time to run stocks down.

Envelopes and labels

There are other stationery costs which you probably would not have incurred before the introduction of the computer. Envelope addressing, for example. The majority of the present generation of computers work best at producing addresses straight on to self-adhesive labels fed through the printer on a tractor drive. To ensure precise registration they have to be manufactured to exacting tolerances with the result that the labels can cost as much as the envelopes themselves. And someone has still to peel them off the backing sheet and stick them on the envelopes (there are machines which will do this, but only, of course, at more expense). Consider what the effect of this extra cost could have on a large mail shot.

Ribbons

Seemingly minor items such as printer ribbons can cost too. As with desks, once an ordinary typewriter ribbon becomes associated with computers, up goes the price.

Maintenance

Computer hardware tends to be reliable once you have it running. If there is a fault on the machine it will probably show up at the outset, and many manufacturers work on a replacement factor much higher than would be tolerated in other industries. However, like all machinery it can break down and, bearing in mind the fact that the computer will, if it is to be effective, have a very high profile within your company, you will want to arrange for instant engineering back-up in the event of a failure.

Despite the reliability of their machines, manufacturers are reluctant to extend guarantees beyond the industry-wide norm of 12 months. Inevitably you will have to take out some form of maintenance contract. Again another cost. All these costs pall into insignificance when compared with the biggest running cost of all — that of getting the information into the computer.

All data, no information!

That's a cry often heard emanating from the lips of many a managing director struggling with a large, unwieldy and above all, powerful data processing department. Underlying it all is the key to any successful computer operation. If the company is to benefit from computers, data must be fed into the system in such a way that it can be turned into information which can be easily understood by those who have to make key decisions based on it. Naturally this calls for a well designed computer program. It also calls for a highly competent set of people feeding in the data in the first place.

And how long will it take to feed all the necessary data into the system to enable you to start using the computer with any degree of confidence? How much data will have to go in? Will details of, say, accounts have to go back 12 months, three years or even back to when the company was formed? Government bodies such as the Inland Revenue can insist on accounts dating back six years or even longer in some cases. Will you put them all on computer (assuming you still have them)? Quantifying this period of start-up is most important. Get it wrong and it will cost you money both in terms of direct costs of the staff feeding the data in and in terms of efficiency lost because you misjudged the time-scale for getting the computer on stream.

Preventing loss of data

And what about contingencies? During the start-up period you will be finding bugs (a bug is computerese for a fault within the computer system, either in the hardware of the computer itself or, more usually, in the software). How much material will be lost if the computer program crashes?

There are ways of keeping consequent losses to a minimum using *back-up* disks. Back-up disks are simply copies of floppy disks used for storing your information. In some computer systems, equipped with two disk drives, a back-up disk can be made automatically; with others you have to instruct the computer to make a copy of a particular disk. It is advisable to back up frequently, particularly if you are doing a long piece of work, all of which could be lost in the event of a power supply failure. Most businesses take the precaution of making security or back-up copies of key disks at the end of each working day. These disks are then taken away from the business premises so the information is secure from break-in or fire damage.

Failure to make back-up disks can result in disaster. At the worst, if you have a fire, or even flood, you could lose the lot. Of course, the same applies to manual records, but remember that the disks on which most of your information will be stored are much more sensitive to a greater number of corrupting influences than ledgers. Not only that, because so much information can be stored on just one small disk, a single disk damaged means that much more information will be lost.

While we're on the subject of losing data, let's look at what happens if it disappears due to a software/hardware malfunction. We should remember that most manufacturers limit their liability to the product itself. They do not hold themselves responsible for consequent losses. If you lose data because their equipment malfunctions, you're on your own. Similarly, in the event of fire or some other catastrophe it is unlikely any insurance company will feel itself to be liable for data losses, unless of course, at more expense, you specifically insure against it. This kind of stark reality tends to concentrate the mind of a would-be computer user. Such is the worry factor, many computer users in business, notably a major international airline, still back up their computer with a manual system. The computer provides the speed of information access they require on a day-to-day basis, but should the system fail the good old ledgers are always there on standby. Most businessmen, though, don't look upon the installation of computers with a view to maintaining their existing manual systems. Perhaps they should. Of course, it doesn't do to concentrate always on the downside, but forewarned is forearmed!

Plan for the future

These days many people are changing their computer systems with increasing frequency. Three years is a long time in the world of the microchip. It is also a long time in the world of a rapidly growing/changing business. Technology moves on; business needs change. Above all, demands for greater capacity, increased and faster access times for computer users expand in direct proportion to the advancement of computer literacy within the company.

As more people in the business chain — both customers and suppliers — acquire computers, the need for interaction between different computers will grow. For some time the potential for every computer terminal to act as its own telex and send messages to other computer owners has been a reality, but *compatibility* remains a problem.

Compatibility is the ability of one computer system to exchange information with other computers. With so many different types of system on the market, all operating in varying ways and all in competition with each other it has been impossible to achieve any cohesive common elements to them which means that the consumer has lost out.

Certainly IBM, holding as it does 75 per cent of the worldwide personal computer market, has been setting some kind of standard. It is their proud boast that every day sees the publication of a new piece of software for their range of personal computers. Software developers are going to make their product available for the biggest slice of the potential market first; others will simply have to coat tail behind.

This does not mean that one is obliged to buy IBM, far from it. There are plenty of other small companies offering faster, more capable machines at a lower price and, with increasing frequency, compatibility with IBM. When the British owned ICL launched their office management computer, One Per Desk, at the beginning of 1985, they took great pains to point out that the machine would link into existing larger computers from other companies as well as their own.

When considering any decision about which system to install you must have an eye to the future. Many computer systems are not truly expandable. Could you really afford equipment redundancy after just a few years?

A better way?

So far you may have found this book pretty chilling reading, particularly this chapter. You may well be deciding that computers are really not worth the effort, or indeed expense. If so, fine, just think of the money you've saved.

What I hope has been achieved so far is to get you to consider all the angles. You might now think that there is a better way forward, but in any event if you do plump for computerisation you will not be going into it unprepared. Perhaps now is not the time; perhaps you want to postpone the decision? Although prices are falling, the real cuts in costs have already occurred. If you start thinking about computers now, and you get your decision train right, then savings made by introducing computers and thus creating greater efficiency should more than compensate for any later reductions in prices.

Case study: Polymedia

Polymedia is a public relations consultancy based in Portsmouth. Much of their work involves circulating trade periodicals, newspapers and broadcasting organisations with news of developments in their clients' businesses. This generally means sending out masses of paper which, although often containing much of the same information in any given press release, does require that 'personal' touch if it is not immediately to be consigned to the waste paper bin. Polymedia's founder and managing director, Sue Todd, decided a word processor was the answer.

> After careful consideration of what was on offer and what we could afford, we opted for the Prospect stand-alone word processor by Philips. We bought, brand new in summer 1983, a dual disk drive version for just over £5,000. To that we added a TEC daisy wheel 40 character per second printer (for us finished copy quality and speed are crucial) for £1,300 which, together with a keyboard and hopper feeder, gave us a hardware package of just over £7,500. We were fortunate in as much as the software was thrown in free by the local agents, although we had to pay over £400 for training. We also opted for a satellite. (A satellite is a computer terminal, but with very little memory or intelligence. It relies on being linked to the main computer. Satellites are sometimes known as 'dumb terminals' and are much cheaper than micro computer terminals proper.) This gave us the facility of having more than one user on the machine at any one time — that was another £1,200.
>
> Shock number one: the cost of maintenance. At slightly over 10 per cent of the purchase price of each item we found we were

paying over £1,000 a year, which makes you wonder whether it is really worthwhile. For us it was worthwhile in the first year just to sort out all the teething troubles. At the beginning of 1984 maintenance charges were raised by nearly 5 per cent and they went up again for 1985. At this point we decided to cut our losses and, for better or worse have resigned our maintenance contract. We now will have to pay a minimum call out charge of £100, with each hour of the engineer's time being invoiced to us at £65.

Shock number two: we very soon discovered that nothing is done 'at the touch of a button'. But once a system is established and working, life is bliss and you keep hearing yourself saying, 'What would we have done without the word processor?'

Lessons to be learned:

1. Allow sufficient time for training; it will always prove worthwhile. Operators cannot absorb every instruction at a single session, so need to be reminded of the short cuts. We also called back our instructors after our first year to check we were using the machine to its full potential.

2. Consider all the uses that may be required of the data before you put it into the computer. One client wanted us to collate the details of a competition draw, involving entries made through over 600 pubs, with competition draws being made on six consecutive weeks. By knowing in advance that they wanted the results in lists by date order, sorted alphabetically according to the winners' names, as well as a list of all winners sorted according to the pub through which they entered, we were able to fulfil the request with ease.

3. Used correctly, such will be the success that you will want to buy more!

At the end of 1984 we purchased another Prospect (a smaller 64K version). A maintenance agreement has been entered into for the first year and has already proved worthwhile in the number of calls to sort out teething troubles. The Philips Prospect is the first word processor to be given British Telecom approval for telex access and we have been investigating how this might help our business.

Chapter 4
The Computer Salesman

The time has now come for you to tackle the computer salesman. They call themselves computer dealers, traders, suppliers, even consultants. They seldom call themselves salesmen. But make no mistake, that is what they are, for the straightforward reason that they make their money out of selling computers. To call them anything else would be to lull ourselves into a false sense of security.

By now you should already have a reasonable amount of scepticism on board. No longer will you be taken in by jargon or clever sales talk, or will you?

High street retailers

From being almost exclusively the preserve of a few large corporations, computers soon became as widely available as television sets. As all computers operate on electricity, when the large computer manufacturers needed to shift vast quantities of hardware it was natural that they should turn to established high street electrical retailers for distribution. So overnight, sharp suited gents who for years had been doing a steady trade in washing machines and refrigerators had suddenly to turn their attention to computers — the coming thing. Well that was all right because, after all, were they not just like television sets? For a start most of the smaller ones needed television sets to operate. What's more, the early predominance of games software packages meant that there was the added sales impetus of a wild-eyed child applying pressure to his poor parents.

Of course, all this seems a long way from business computers, but it's as well to consider the background to the general boom in computers because, as the market for games-based computers becomes saturated — and there are signs that saturation point is already being reached — the pressure mounts to sell up-market systems, many of them on the threshold of business usage. True, some salesmen are already returning to their washing machines and fridges, but many, particularly as their retailing employers have already cut a good slice of the computer cake, are being encouraged to bone up on the new generations of computers. Witness the number of high street names who are now boasting computer 'centres'. Some do try to make these genuinely separate entities — real 'shops within shops'. Others, unfortunately, use their computers to brighten up some dark corner of the premises down among the television sets and stereo systems.

The trouble from the salesman's point of view is that there's a lot more to know about computers than there is, say, about a fridge. Everyone knows what you put in a fridge; try applying that analogy to a computer. Lack of knowledge of the equipment is only part of the problem; the average salesman will be able to make most computers function to a level reasonable enough to impress the casual buyer. But the real problems arise from the average salesman's lack of knowledge about business matters. There is a quantum leap from selling a washing machine on the promise of domestic bliss to selling a fully fledged business computer which guarantees super management efficiency.

The first rule of buying your system is to know what kind of establishment to go to. So is the high street altogether the wrong place to go in search of a business computer? In the past, the answer would have been yes, but things are getting better. You need to be sure of back-up, of which more later. A high street trader with a high profile reputation to maintain could well have more reason to look sympathetically on the problems created by a machine he sold you. The other advantage is that, by virtue of the plurality of the electrical devices he sells, he's probably been in business far longer than the average specialist computer dealer and as such is less likely (but not definitely) to go bust. You may also find the very high street position of the shop attractive in terms of convenience but that is unlikely to be a major factor in choosing your dealer.

There are, though, very many reasons *not* to go to a high street trader. The fact that he sells a number of systems may, in the initial stages of the buying process, be an advantage in as much as you can see under one roof a greater spread of machines, but after that it is a positive disadvantage. The high street dealer will simply not have the breadth of knowledge among his staff to give you the in-depth answers to the questions you need to ask (we'll be looking at what those questions might be a little later).

Many of the bigger computer manufacturers have seized the

So You Think Your Business Needs a Computer?

point about product knowledge. IBM, for example, make great play of the hoops their dealers have to go through before they are awarded their much coveted dealerships. Similarly, ICL have developed a quite considerable marketing thrust behind their 'Traderpoint' concept. And it's the same for other hardware companies such as ACT (Apricot) and Apple. So it looks as though the specialists win the day when it comes to computers for business.

If you ever wanted proof of that consider what happened to me a few years ago when, flush with both enthusiasm for getting into the computing world and around £2,000 burning a hole in my pocket, I sallied forth into a number of high streets over a period of several weeks determined to buy my way into the computer age. I visited electrical shops one after another all boasting big ranges of computer hardware and software. Some salesmen were very well informed about the intrinsic qualities of the hardware on offer: 'Oh yes, 64K RAM fully expandable with cartridge ROM packages on stream very shortly.' Sadly, when it came to business applications it soon became apparent that they were greatly out of their depth. Many were not long out of school so it was perhaps unreasonable to expect much knowledge of the trials and tribulations of the world of business. Their older colleagues tended to nod knowingly when I outlined some of the business areas I wanted to computerise, but began to get a distinctly glazed look when I started to delve deeper into the availability of software packages and the like.

Of course, there were exceptions; one salesman almost got to the point of parting me from my money! He almost persuaded me to buy for business use a system based on the BBC micro. It's an admirable machine for educational purposes, but hardly the best value for money when it comes to a business application. Incredibly I had made the decision to have the system in under half an hour and on a verbal assurance only, that comprehensive business software, suitable for the needs I had outlined was available. The salesman was only able to show me a fraction of the software necessary because that was all he had in stock. Fortunately, he was short of a disk drive unit, so in the end I decided not to go through the process of waiting for the device to be ordered etc.

I was saved from making a costly mistake, ironically by the very lack of instant sales availability that the retail computer market has built its business on. Because I could not have the hardware there and then the sale failed to complete; I wanted my boxes of goodies instantly. As I said that was a few years ago — I know better now, I hope!

Finding the right dealer

By this stage we shall assume that, chastened by my experience in the high street and other horror stories, you will be heading for your local specialist dealer. It is likely that you will by now be veering towards some of the big names in the business computer world. IBM is well ahead of the others — Commodore, Apple, ICL, ACT, and the fast rising Japanese manufacturers. The trouble is that you are unlikely to find more than two or three of the big names under one roof. None of the big manufacturers wants a conflict of interests in the showrooms of their cherished dealers. So you will probably have to seek out and visit at least three separate dealers, but that is no bad thing. That way you compare not only the machines but also the dealers, and as Christopher Goodhart of the Olive Tree Trading Company points out when, in the final analysis he came to choosing a computer for his business, it was what he described as 'empathy with the dealer' that swung the whole deal (see the case study on page 79).

Once you have located your dealers (if you have difficulty the head offices of all the big computer manufacturers should be able to help you) make sure you allow plenty of time to visit them. A couple of hours ought to be ample in the first instance, but certainly no less than an hour for the initial meeting. Resist the temptation to let him come and visit you at this stage, even if he suggests it. Remember you may end up trusting a good deal of your company's future to his efforts. You at least want to know how he operates. In any event, he ought to be much better placed to show you what his particular range of machines are capable of on his home ground. You will also, being experienced in business, be able to get a measure of his operation at first hand.

One management consultant I know, specialising in improving production efficiency, swears he can tell quite a lot about the state of a firm by its lavatories. A filthy loo means a lackadaisical company. You may want to add other, perhaps more scientific, analyses to this rather basic management technique, but the basic point is well made.

The next point is, even for the very first meeting, don't go

So You Think Your Business Needs a Computer?

alone. If you are following an enlightened policy of consultation with your staff, choose a staff representative to go with you. You will be surprised how useful this can be.

Let us pause to consider the questions that should be asked (we will assume that you have given the salesman a clear idea about what *you* are expecting from the computer):

1. In the salesman's experience how easy is it to introduce a system suitable to your needs into the business?
2. How long will it take before the computer is fully 'on stream'?
3. What are the pitfalls when it comes to training staff to use the machine?
4. What is the best software to achieve the desired result?
5. What are the alternatives?
6. Are they cheaper/more expensive?
7. What is the best hardware to work with the software?
8. What are the alternatives?
9. Are they cheaper/more expensive?
10. Who will install the system — the dealership, engineers from the hardware manufacturers or an independent third party such as a computer consultancy?
11. Who will be responsible for maintaining the system?
12. What are the costs — of software, hardware and maintenance? Can these be put in writing?
13. What about spare parts and stationery — is there security of supply?
14. Will the computer system expand to meet the growing needs of your business or will you have to exchange it for another?

This list is by no means exhaustive but it's a good start. It is important to stress how useful it can be to have members of staff accompanying you. They will often ask far more penetrating questions than you might have thought of. This is for several reasons. The first is that, while you may have already made up *your* mind to introduce computers, there may still be doubts lingering in the minds of some staff and there's nothing like a lingering doubt to hone the critical faculties. Apart from that, a member of staff at the sharp end is undoubtedly better placed to outline the unique problems faced by your business and then spot difficulties and potential hiccups in the operational procedures being advanced by the computer salesman. It usually turns out that it's the staff member who is least likely to let the computer salesman off the hook.

How big is their byte?

A byte is the term used for the amount of computer 'memory' needed to store one letter of text. The capacity of a computer system is measured in thousands of bytes or kilobytes.

From the very outset you have to get a measure of the computer sales person you are dealing with; you have to sort out the sheep from the goats. But how do you do this when, by definition, the good man is going to know more about computer systems than you ever will? Surely he will be able to dazzle you with his computer-based brilliance, and you will be in no position to argue? Perhaps, but a really good salesman will want to hear from you what you think your computer system should achieve, even if that view is modified later. First of all, do not hold back. You're in the driving seat. You don't want to be bogged down with jargon, taken for a fool or, horror of horrors, sold a pup. All you want is a computer to make your life easier. A good computer man will accept that it is up to him to help you define your needs as they apply to your business and not according to what he has on offer in his showroom.

First, let's test our salesman by checking out his overview. Ask him what he thinks about the competition. This way you'll be able to get a sense of how much he understands about the computers he is selling and how much they relate to business needs. Watch out for evasive or dismissive answers. If he's evasive, he probably doesn't know much about the competition; and if he doesn't know the competition he probably doesn't really have a true understanding of the good and bad points of the machines he is selling. If he's dismissive, he might well know about the competition, but could it be that, far from being worthy of dismissal, a competitor's offering might just be better than what he has to offer? As in war, in a sales operation, often the first casualty is truth.

Most computer systems have good and bad points. A good computer salesman should be able to compare and contrast the main competitors fairly honestly. He should also be prepared to admit when he has no knowledge or experience of a particular system, but few computer salesmen do. If yours does, cling to him, you have discovered an honest man!

Now you have got him talking about the various hardware on the market, his own and the competition's, throw a spanner in the works and ask about the software. So far in this chapter we have been discussing hardware to the virtual exclusion of all else whereas earlier in the book I stressed that software is king. Unfortunately computer dealers are still very much hardware led. The reason for this is quite simply that only the big hardware manufacturers have had the resources to set up dealership networks so vital to the distribution of their products. Even the big software houses such as Lotus have had to climb into bed with major hardware companies like IBM in order to secure a good foothold in the market. There are signs that some of this is changing but only in as much as some hardware companies, most notably IBM, are seeking the advantages in developing in-house software to go with the hardware.

Why didn't they get into software before? Remember their history. IBM stands for International Business Machines; traditionally they made typewriters and adding machines requiring primarily engineering-based skills. The kind of brain power that is essential to software development was not initially available in-house. Not only that, they had large factories to keep in production, so the pressure was on to keep selling the boxes.

Inevitably you will have to prise your dealer away from trying to sell you one of his machines to talking about the software. His knowledge of software is the key to his competence. It will be very tempting for him to extol the virtues of the systems he has to sell regardless of how well they fit into your individual requirements. This you will have to resist. The secret of success in your quest for a perfect computer system is to invest in an operation where both hardware and software match your precise needs. It's a tall order but not insurmountable.

Let us now assume that your dealer is talking fluently about the range of software packages his machines will run with. Hit him once again with a few more punchy questions. Which, in his experience, are the best selling and therefore most successful packages? Will he give you the name and address of someone who is successfully using a system based on hardware and software supplied by him? Would he be prepared to visit your business to see at first hand the problems involved? The answers to all these questions ought to be yes. Conceivably, he might want to caveat the second by asking to consult with a current customer before giving you his name and address, but that should only serve to confirm the care and esteem he holds for his clients. You represent potential sales of thousands of pounds to him so he should want to deal.

Beware any dealer who at this stage tries to railroad you into an instant decision. Not many should at this level, as all the main product knowledge courses run by the big hardware companies stress their abhorrence of their machines being sold under pressure. They know from bitter experience that such a sales policy only stores up resentment and trouble for the future. A good salesman will appreciate how big a step computerisation represents to you and ought gracefully to allow you the time to think it over.

He will try to fix a date to visit you there and then. If you're so minded then by all means make the appointment, but try to allow yourself time to fit in a visit or two, or at least a phone call, to those satisfied customers he's just told you about. The next time you meet, you want to be at least one jump ahead of the game. You will by now have gained some kind of impression of the man, the operation, the machines he has on offer. If any of them give you cause for concern, don't fix another appointment, just tell him you have a lot of factors to consider and you'll get back to him.

There is little more that you can or indeed should, achieve at this first meeting. It is time to depart and mull over what you have learnt. Try to write down the plus and minus points of what you've seen. They should include the following:

1. Did the salesman appear to know what he was talking about?
2. Did he grasp what your particular business needs were?
3. Did he offer credible solutions to those needs in terms of both hardware and software?
4. Was he able to discuss systems other than those he had to sell?
5. Was he prepared to take time to allow you to consider the alternatives, or did he try to rush you into a decision?
6. Was he realistic about the potential costs involved?
7. From your brief visit did the company 'feel' right; could you trust the salesman?

This is another occasion where consulting with a member of staff will pay dividends. If possible get him or her to write up the meeting separately and then compare notes. Repeat this with your other dealers and then do three things:

1. Take soundings from all relevant levels within the firm.
2. Take up any references supplied by computer firms of current users of their systems (you'll be amazed at how open people are about their computers. During the writing of this book I

found everyone had a computer story to tell; it was almost like discussing health, with people just dying to show you their operation scars!).
3. Take plenty of time to think about the next step.

Come, see, conquer!

Many computer salesmen see the visit to a client's business as a challenge. You should not discourage this view. In fact this is the one opportunity really to impress upon him how privileged he is even to be considered for supplying computer equipment to your firm. You want to use the visit to get him first to understand your operation with its unique business needs and problems, and also to realise that if his system does not come up to scratch how many people he will be letting down. On the first point, you and your fellow managers will be well placed to give an overview of your operation and the demands you will be making on any computer system in management terms. Once you have achieved that, let the staff loose on him. If you've been involved in consultation you will, over a period of many months, have been subjected to the full brunt of resentment, suspicion and distrust that seems to accompany any proposal aimed at introducing new technology. Give your staff someone else to bray at; see how he stands up to it. After all he ought to have all the answers.

You may want to put more than one salesman through this process. After each visit get a view from your staff about what they think about the salesman. Did he quickly grasp the points they were making? How did he react to sharp criticism? Was he too dismissive of the potential problems in, for example, training? Was he too glib about the capabilities of the system? Do the staff like him?

This last question is perhaps the most important. This man could continue to be a contact long after the computer system is installed. He may even be the person who comes to do the training course. Staff have got to like and trust him; even relatively small points have to be spotted. I remember a case where training seemed to be getting nowhere until the real cause of the difficulty was identified. It turned out that the salesman, who also came to do the training, had the most unconscionable body odour. Potential computer operators would move heaven and earth to get out of their training sessions closeted in a small computer room with the man. Yes indeed, if anyone can sniff out problems with your computer man, your staff will!

With the visit to your business complete you should now let the computer salesman make the next move. He may want further visits, or to send some of his colleagues along to help assess the needs of your operation. If he asks for this, do not unnecessarily deny it to him although you would be quite justified in getting an estimate of time-scale from him. The imperative of wanting to sell you a system should keep his eye on the ball but it is as well to know how the design and set-up of the system is progressing. You can only do this if you have some kind of time-scale (albeit one set by him) against which to measure developments.

Before you part with any money, you should expect to see a *specification* and *estimate* for both hardware and software, tailored to your business. These should be in writing and should be clear and concise. You will have started off with your own specification of what you believe your business needs from computerisation and during your consultations with the computer supplier this will have been modified to take account of factors raised during discussions.

The written specification supplied by the computer company prior to your placing the order should be given wide circulation among interested parties in your company at all levels (you may decide to circulate the specification without the financial details). When dealing with computers it is important to get as many brains inputting into the decision-making process as possible. Discuss the specification in-house once everyone has had a chance to read it. Highlight any points that need greater clarification. If necessary invite the computer salesman to explain or amplify such points. This is often a good opportunity for the salesman to bring along some of the hardware for the staff to try 'hands on'. You might discover certain practical difficulties about, say, the keyboards (of which more in a later chapter).

If everyone is happy, you can then move to the final stage of the deal.

Deal yourself a good hand

In this closing stage of the negotiation you really want to tie down your salesman so that he has no doubts about what you are expecting from him. The specification must be clearly defined. You will want to know delivery dates, bearing in mind that with the installation of a computer system you will first face the physical upheaval of the equipment being moved in, and then the potentially much bigger upset of trying to get the computer up and running with your staff and your systems. It needs careful planning. We agreed earlier that attempting to transfer all aspects of the company's systems to computer in one go is pure folly, so what will you go for first? In consultation with your computer supplier you need to timetable a list of priorities. This will be based on a combination of what you see as top priority and the computer man's knowledge of which systems usually present the most difficulty. For example, stock control may well be your biggest headache. Many people would argue that to make that your first installation module would court disaster because of the complexities of stock control systems. Remember the importance of maintaining staff morale. The last thing you want to do is have the computer or its operating staff fall at the first fence. Far better to concentrate on a relatively simple module first off. Start with invoicing say, then sales and purchase ledgers, moving through into nominal ledger and so on.

Confirm the installation details. Will the computer supplier be handling all aspects of getting the computers on line? It is not unreasonable for him to expect power sockets to be conveniently available, but what if the computer terminals are to form a networked system or make use of telephone links? (A networked system is where a number of computers are linked together so they can share information and in some cases software programs. They can be linked together by their own dedicated wires which have to be installed specially, or they can use existing telephone connections and link with each other through the PABX.) Will you have to plan and organise that? Is that another cost you hadn't considered?

Once the system is installed, how long will the supplier need for debugging (getting rid of minor faults which always seem to arise when a computer system is installed)? Will the training be in-house or will staff have to attend courses elsewhere? Can you build in a six- or twelve-month ongoing consultation period to help sort out problems as they arise? And what about guarantees for the equipment itself? We have already discovered that few computer suppliers will take responsibility for consequential loss, let's at least make sure the hardware is covered. There's a lot to be tied up but nothing must be left to chance.

A better way?

Throughout this chapter we have been discussing the purchase and installation of a computer system as if the only way forward was through the appointed dealers of the big hardware manufacturers. In the main, the dealership networks are set up to give a good geographical spread, so you have a fair chance of getting a supplier who is really local to you. This is an important factor, for if things start to go wrong with your system, the supplier is likely to be even less inclined to visit you to sort it out if he has to drive several miles each time. By going to an appointed dealer you will also, in theory at least, get some kind of guarantee relating to the dealer's probity. The big companies are not too keen on handing out dealerships to firms who don't have the necessary financial or technical backing. The computer industry is still very young and track record is still an elusive quality.

There is a major drawback, though, to following the course outlined here. Because you are going to a supplier who makes his real profit from selling boxes of hardware, all decisions are inevitably going to be led by the availability of the equipment. The software will almost always be selected after the hardware, and we have agreed in earlier chapters that it should really be the other way around. Fortunately it is getting easier to achieve software-led computerisation, and that is what we shall discuss next.

The computer contract

You may need to check some or all of the following points when entering into a computer contract; they are drawn to the attention of businessmen by 3i (Investors in Industry) and will mean more to you by the time you reach the end of this book.

1. Identify the parties to the contract.
2. Describe carefully the subject matter, with reference to the supplier's proposals and literature.
3. State location. Consider the inclusion of an alternative location.
4. Price. State the total price; deposits and instalments; discounts; increases or reviews; costs of services and any ancillary charges.

So You Think Your Business Needs a Computer?

5. Details of payment.
6. Delivery.
7. Timing, also duration and renewal of limited period agreements.
8. Performance standards.
9. Staff recruitment (if this forms part of the agreement only).
10. Communication structure between the parties.
11. Definition of technical and frequently used terms.
12. Use. The supplier should specify standards and requirements for using the subject matter, and avoid placing restrictions on using other equipment, software and services.
13. Consider whether limitations on the user will affect possible business developments.
14. Maintenance. Confirm the supplier's responsibility and avoid conflict between provisions of different maintenance agreements. Nature, standard, period, price, procedures etc.
15. Services provided to user, if any.
16. Regarding the hardware purchase: equipment identification, capacity and performance in relation to other (stated) considerations, suitability and quality, replacement, compatibility, installation and commissioning, standby facilities, physical and environmental requirements, improvements (for future development if required), trade in.
17. Regarding software licences: period of licence, termination arrangements, likely developments in the software, possible changes in the organisation's systems, charges, identification of each program and its capabilities, new versions, support and error correction, documentation to be kept up to date by supplier, acceptance testing, rights in custom-written software and/or amendments to standard software.
18. Legal points.

Chapter 5

Software First

There is a growing body of opinion among computer experts with no axe to grind that the selection of hardware can really be left until suitable software packages have been specified for the task required. It's true that you will need the hardware but it need not be the primary consideration when introducing computerisation to a business. This view is backed up by the experience of many business people who, relatively early in the computer revolution, jumped in at the deep end and very nearly drowned. In many cases their businesses nearly went down as well.

This feeling that software has always played Cinderella to hardware is borne out by the rise of a whole range of computer consultants displacing the cowboys who jump on the bandwagon of any new, rapidly expanding area of commerce. The advent of the consultant has been a godsend to the business world, but only in as much as businesses have been able to choose who they want to advise them on computerisation. So how do you make the correct choice of adviser? What information do you need?

Software is the name given to the information fed into the hardware (the computer) that tells it how to do the tasks required. It is the link between the brains of you, your colleagues and your staff and the brain of the computer housed in the hardware. Without it you are nowhere. The trouble is that good software is more difficult to spot than good hardware.

With hardware you may feel inclined to make a value judgement based on the 'look' of the product, the feel of the keyboard, the clarity of the visual display unit (VDU) and so on. It would be reasonable to argue that if a manufacturer had spent time and money on producing an attractive computer he would also, although by no means necessarily, have put a lot of effort into the functioning of the hardware. With software it's different. The product is likely to consist of little more than a couple of floppy disks, and although many software houses do spend money on packaging software as attractively as possible (software packages for the retail trade are often launched with over £10,000-worth of design input) it is hard to make floppy disks look more than they really are.

As well as examining the floppy disks (described on page 82) you could also look at the accompanying manuals. A well written manual could mean good, well thought out software, but as with hardware, it isn't necessarily so.

What you are buying with software is intelligence — intelligence in a form you can easily understand and which can easily be applied to your business, its staff, and its operating systems.

The software consultant's role

The software consultant is the man who has set himself up to help you identify the right kind of software intelligence for your operation. His sales pitch is (or should be) that he can bridge all the gaps in your knowledge, help to fill the cracks in your experience and act as the fount of all wisdom when it comes to you and your computer system. In short the consultant should, at a stroke, relieve you of the headaches associated with computerisation. Unlike the average computer salesman consultants should not, at the outset at least, be keen to offer an easy 'one shot' solution to your problem which just happens to be the latest machine he has on offer for a limited period only. It is often said that the computer salesman is selling solutions in search of problems; the software consultant ought to be prepared to identify the problem first and only then search for a suitable solution.

Who are these consultants?

In the main there are two types of software consultant. The first tends to be a one-man band. He will have had training in computer programming and have worked as a programmer, either for a hardware manufacturer, as an in-house programmer in the data processing department of a large company, or as a programmer in a software development company. I say 'have worked'; he may still be working for another employer and trying to strike out on his own as a consultant on a part-time basis: not that there's anything intrinsically wrong with this. A computer consultant who shows that kind of entrepreneurial spirit could be just what you are looking for.

There is another category of consultant who offers a one-man service. He's the student who offers consultancy in return for an opportunity to develop a system, if only on paper, for a real live business, usually as a project for his computer course. Such a consultant has both advantages and disadvantages.

The advantage is that he comes to your business fresh and, in theory, unprejudiced, except for the teachings of his computer lecturer who no doubt will have inculcated his own set of judgements on computer systems. Because of his youth, it's possible he will spot ways in which computerisation can help your business, but here may come the first drawback to using a 'student consultant'. It is unlikely he will have much knowledge of the needs of a business and therefore it may take him longer to reach conclusions about suitable computer systems. He will also be untrammelled by considerations of cost and so, as in the case of the Olive Tree Trading Company (see page 79) may recommend a system beyond the company's means.

You may feel that, bearing in mind the difficulties of employing a 'student consultant', a company would be unwise even to consider such a possibility.

One obvious way of minimising the risk of employing a computer 'non-professional' is to take on not the student, but his teacher. Here you trade experience and wisdom for the flexibility and economy of youth. In short, the computer lecturer will cost you more, but he should be able to draw on greater expertise than a student and be more likely to come up with the correct computer solution for your business.

Many businesses have reported a favourable outcome from both courses of action, though these cases seem to be few and far between and, where students are involved, of the 'boss's son' variety.

'We got this computer in the office. No one could work it until my son came home on his summer holidays. In two weeks he had all the payroll running on it, stock control and reordering a couple of weeks later. The people who supplied the computer were so amazed, they even offered him a job!'

Such stories probably owe more to paternal pride, combined with a perhaps natural antipathy towards so-called experts, than to any lasting achievement in computer programming. What is our proud entrepreneurial father going to do when the system crashes? Bring his son racing back from college to sort out the problem?

So You Think Your Business Needs a Computer?

The chief attraction of using a student is cost, which brings me to the main point when considering a software-led computer installation. Without question it will be expensive, but if you make the right decisions, you gain much more for your money than just a computer.

The one-man computer consultant does, on the face of it, represent a relatively inexpensive way of arriving at the right solutions for your computer problems.

Let us now look at another category of one-man consultant, the programmer who has worked for a hardware manufacturer. He will probably be good. The big hardware companies tend only to recruit the brightest and the best. If he has wanted to branch out on his own, all well and good — there is nothing wrong with showing a little entrepreneurial spirit. However, you need to know more about what he actually did within the programming department of his computer company. If he worked solely on the operating systems of computers, then he may have little knowledge that will help him when it comes to recommending, adapting or writing software for your business operations. On the other hand, if he was attached to, say, the marketing department, analysing and testing new software packages for their suitability to the company's hardware, then he will have a lot of very useful knowledge indeed.

I often think that the ideal person to have would be the one who tests all the software packages written for the IBM range of personal computers as they come on to the market, although I very much doubt if all such testing is placed in the hands of just one individual. The fact that such consultants' experience would be restricted to the hardware of their former employers could be a severe drawback.

If we consider the next option, the programmer who has worked, or is still working, in the data processing department of a large company, we need to ask ourselves whether the individual will be hidebound by 'large company' solutions. Large companies tend to go for a belt and braces style of computerisation on the grounds that, where a centralised data processing department is serving a large group of companies, the costs of installing back-up or even tandem systems can be justified by spreading the costs across the group. Smaller businesses are usually looking for the most economical, rather than a gold plated solution to their problems. Additionally, the larger machines and their software can be very different from the range of smaller computer systems favoured by small and medium-sized businesses. You will need to know more about your would-be consultant's experience in the areas that apply to your business.

You are on a much better wicket altogether with the consultant who comes to you from a software development house. He should be well up to date with the latest packages, as all software developers take great pains to ensure that they keep abreast of the competition. He also ought to have first-hand knowledge of the problems faced by businesses trying to write software packages for their own specific business needs, or trying to adapt existing software to suit unique business applications. But again, it is wise to check in detail that his experience is relevant to your field of operation. If, for example, you are a solicitor who wants a sophisticated word processing package with access to databases of legal precedents, judgements and case law, often through international bureaux such as EuroLex, then you need someone who really knows the ins and outs of word processing software. If your consultant's experience has hitherto been limited to installing an accounts package along with an off-the-peg word processing package, it's likely he won't be able to offer you the depth of experience you need.

The secret is to check thoroughly the credentials of your would-be consultant.

Consultancies

So far we have talked exclusively of the one-man band consultants. There are others, and they tend to be manned by business people who have made a business of consultancy. Often they will have started out as one-man band outfits and built their business to the point where they can employ others. The good ones always make a point of identifying themselves personally with the consultancy service their firm offers. Computer consultancy is very much a personal affair. The businessman must feel he has one single point of contact when something goes wrong, and most will not settle for that person being anyone other than the boss, and quite rightly so.

This need for personal identification naturally puts constraints of size on such software consultancy businesses. Depending on the management skills of the person at the top, it is unlikely that the operation will be able to maintain the personal touch if the organisation grows to much more than a dozen or 15 employees, but there are exceptions.

As with the categories of individual consultant one must examine carefully the credentials of the consultancy and check in detail what is being offered. This is easier if you are dealing with a large consultancy, likely to have a longer track record on which you can make your judgement. Such is the newness of the consultancy game, with a few exceptions most firms will have been established in the business less than five years. Quite simply, you will not have the information to make a proper judgement or indeed the time to carry out a proper analysis. So, how to choose? Well, there is really only one way that gives any degree of certainty about the computer consultant, whether he be a one-man band, or larger firm: the likelihood is you will have to fall back on that tried and tested business standby, *recommendation*.

Recommended consultants

Recommendation can save you an awful lot of time and effort, but can also be a pretty hit-and-miss affair if you are not careful. Too often the recommendation comes from a business associate who may have had different computer problems from yours, for which his blue-eyed consultant may not have the relevant experience. So even though recommendation may save you a lot of worry, it would be unwise to suspend all your judgemental faculties. Where recommendation can be a boon is in getting in advance some idea of how your consultant is going to turn out in the long term.

1. Does he have leanings towards any particular hardware company?
2. How does he approach training?
3. Does he have the diligence you would expect when it comes to maintenance and trouble shooting once the computer system is up and running?

You can get a fair impression of all these factors by simply talking to the person who is making the recommendation. It follows that recommendation is a fairly widespread method of finding a computer consultant. Indeed most good software consultants maintain that more than 90 per cent of their business comes from recommendation. Many have even stopped advertising. They find the best advertisement for their services is a satisfied customer who makes a point of spreading the word among his business associates. There is no doubt that, although this branch of the computer world is still very much in its infancy, there are enough consultants who have been around for a reasonable amount of time together with enough satisfied (and dissatisfied) customers to make recommendation the best way of finding a consultant.

Who needs a consultant?

Let us pause awhile and consider once again why you should want to acquire your computer system with the help of a consultant. The alternative is to wander round the various hardware-based companies and buy a well advertised, tried and tested machine and use an off-the-peg range of software recommended for it. Many companies have done just that and a proportion of them have claimed considerable success with this approach. If, for example, your company is relatively young, it is possible to introduce an off-the-peg accountancy system that can be easily married into the existing operation.

It is often argued that computerisation can be most effective when introduced in the first two years of a company's existence, before the company, its operating systems and staff, get too set in their ways. With thousands of new firms being formed every year there is clearly going to be a market for off-the-peg systems for some time to come. It's different for established firms where the computer will have to face all the human emotions associated with innovation. Here there will have to be much more flexibility, probably for the most part on the side of the computer and its software. It's the same too, albeit to a lesser extent, for a young firm which started out with an off-the-peg system, but which now wants to adapt and change to take account of expansion or variation in trading circumstances.

In these cases consultants, in particular software consultants, come into their own. It is a mistake to underestimate the potential problems with off-the-peg systems. It will be fine when you follow the manual to the letter, but inevitably you will spot a short cut which, not unreasonably, you would expect the software to be able to implement with little difficulty.

The trouble is, off-the-peg software is of necessity designed with generalism in mind: if you like, the lowest common business denominator. In itself it is not set up to take account of the subtler nuances of your particular business operation. No doubt the computer salesman who sold you the software together with the hardware would have told you, had you asked him about it at the time, that the software could be modified to take account of your particular needs. But who is going to do it? Certainly not you; you have neither the skill nor the experience and certainly not the time to start trying to rewrite the software program. Nor is it likely that any of your staff will either.

The computer salesman may be someone who specialised in selling washing machines until a couple of years ago, so he won't have the knowledge. If he is genuinely knowledgeable about his products he may not have the time or not see a real profit in such an undertaking when compared with the margins and commissions available to him for selling boxes of computer hardware.

He may recommend you to a software development house or a computer consultant, but then the argument has come full circle except for the fact that you will be going to your consultant almost 'cap in hand' rather than from a position of strength. Often, the attitude of the consultant will be similar to that of an authorised motor car agent to whom you have taken your car after poor servicing by a back street, but inexpensive, unauthorised garage. Apart from giving you a hard time, the consultant, like a plumber called out on a bank holiday weekend, is likely to charge punitively for his services. What's more, if something subsequently goes wrong, he will be well placed, if somewhat unjustifiably, to blame the problem on the original hardware/software combination.

In short, if you think your business will merit any kind of special software modification, then the consultancy route should seriously be considered. It will cost you more money, but it could save you a considerable amount of money and anxiety in the long run.

Measure their mettle

Choosing a software consultant involves many of the same factors outlined in Chapter 4 on the computer salesman. In general terms, the big difference between a software consultant and the computer salesman is that while the latter will tend to have little depth of knowledge or experience of computers and rely on the back-up of the big hardware companies, the consultant should be very well versed in computers and software. It is unlikely he will know enough about all applications of computers, so check exactly what his knowledge amounts to. Ask for references from businesses similar to yours and make enquiries. Phone calls to three or four of these should establish his credentials. Remember, if his advice is bad you probably won't be able to fall back on support by a large organisation. What you are looking for is knowledge applicable to your business. His lack of big company backing is compensated for by the fact that he will be independent of the 'big boys' of the computer world.

You will have to satisfy yourself as to the soundness of his own business. You want your consultant to be around for a long time and the last thing you need is for him to set up your computer system and then to go bust. Check when you take up references about his computing knowledge that he has no disputes in progress which could send him under. Another factor in ensuring his solvency is to pay him. Make sure you are prepared to do this promptly.

The consultant should be able to tackle not only the software needs of your business, but from those recommend suitable hardware. But just because you are paying a fee to an expert does not mean you can just 'leave it all to him'. As with the computer salesman it is important to involve the consultant in the consultative process; it is vital that he and his team (where applicable) hit it off with your staff. They are going to be working too closely together for it to be any other way.

At this initial stage it might be worth inviting, say, three consultants to 'pitch' competitively for the job of bringing computerisation to your firm. Let them each set about discovering how your company operates and identifying its computer needs. Such is the competition in the computer world that most consultants would welcome the chance to pitch for the work, unless of course they happen to be very good, very busy or both.

This kind of competition would also allow you to consider other categories of consultant. The computer manufacturers have taken great pains to attract the best people in the field into their respective dealer networks. This is a direct response to recognition of the need for good advice before a purchase, and back-up once a computer has been installed. Some good people, many of them former consultants, have been attracted by the large salaries on offer. It might be worth giving them a chance to see what they make of your company's computer challenge, but only as part of a competitive arrangement. Most people will undertake a general survey and analysis combined with a proposal and costing on a speculative basis, putting in more or less time depending on the size of contract they are likely to get out of a successful bid.

The one drawback with this kind of competitive tender arrangement is that consultants will justifiably argue that they can only come up with an accurate analysis and proposal after spending a considerable amount of time assessing the business. It's a classic Catch 22; they only sell their time and to give it away in such a manner would not be cost effective for them in the long run. However, it should be possible to get something on paper on which an assessment can be made.

Your best allies in selecting the right man for the job are likely to be your staff (if you are a company that is; if you are a one-man band or partnership, then you will have to rely on the wisdom of yourself and/or your colleagues). They will have had a chance to talk to the man while he's been carrying out his preliminary assessment. Let them see the submitted proposals (minus the costs if you like) and get their views about each. It may be that you settle for one individual overall but like one or two suggestions made by other consultants. There is no reason why, with suitable diplomacy, you should not discuss such suggestions with your chosen consultant.

In an ideal world the best consultant on software and hardware would be one who has no axe to grind on behalf of a manufacturer; one who has a breadth of knowledge covering the whole range of computer systems open to you. Sadly, such individuals are hard to come by; even the most impartial will have a leaning towards the systems he has most knowledge of, probably those he was trained on, in the same way as people have a soft spot for their first car. Integrity is an important factor when choosing a consultant — another reason for putting the consultancy 'out to tender'.

When you eventually choose your consultant, you may feel inclined to make some kind of payment to the unsuccessful consultants for any major ideas of theirs you subsequently use, although there is of course no enforceable copyright on ideas.

Now you have settled for your consultant, it's time to talk turkey.

The price is right?

We have already discussed and probably accepted that computerisation through a consultant is going to cost you more than buying an off-the-peg computer hardware and software system. How much more will depend on what you require of your consultant. Certain costs are relatively fixed, namely the hardware, together with peripherals (see Chapter 16) and stationery. They can be quantified as soon as the software decision is made. A range of hardware can be considered, and even when the software is in a relatively early stage of its development, estimated figures for hardware and associated costs can be worked out and inserted into the computerisation budget.

It is more difficult to predict what the software development costs are likely to be. Initially your consultant should operate in exactly the same way as the computer salesman (see Chapter 4), but analysing your business and its operating systems in greater depth, with consequent dividends in efficiency, because he should know only too well the importance of understanding the business before specifying the software.

Once he has discussed the situation with you and your staff, he should draw up a document breaking down areas of computerisation, together with a list of priorities, and have them approved by you; he will then take one of three routes. He will either recommend the development of a software package specifically tailored to your needs, or he will match the brief to an existing off-the-peg system, or he will modify an existing system. Let us consider each in turn.

1. Writing software from scratch can be expensive; certainly it is the most costly option of the three. If your business has unique operations, it's as well to get an equally unique piece of software. For example, a trout farm needed to analyse accurately the feed intake in order to manage the operation better and cut down on wastage. This meant details of literally hundreds of feeds a day being fed into the computer. This data would be stored for a couple of weeks and then used to update graphical displays of feeding trends as measured against live weight gain. Once in that form the data was dumped from the bottom to make way for more information coming in at the top. It was important, though, to keep the data for a couple of weeks in case of any catastrophe which might have been feed related. Accessing relevant data

within a two-week period was therefore important. A sophisticated software package was needed and as this was the first trout farm to undertake such detailed analysis, it had to be written from scratch.

2. Off-the-peg software, as we have already discussed, is designed to meet a wide range of requirements in the business world if only to guarantee the package a large enough market to make it profitable. You may feel that if you are paying out for a consultant to advise you and all he comes up with is a package which you could have walked in and bought from a computer shop yourself, you have been cheated. Don't forget, when you buy the off-the-peg package, that you are taking the risk of it not being right for the job. If the consultant takes the risk then it's his neck on the line. That is what you are paying him for. It is a brave, if honest, consultant who recommends an off-the-peg package. It should be remembered, though, that when it comes to such packages the consultant may have access to, and knowledge of, software not generally available, some of it written by his own company.

3. It is much more likely that your consultant will come up with a solution based on an off-the-peg package, suitably modified. This offers the best of both worlds: a package tailored to your needs minus the costs associated with bespoke systems. It must be stressed that what matters above all is that you get something which works. Penny pinching at this stage will serve only to store up trouble for the future which might cost you much more to fix. Once you are locked into computerisation you can be saddled with considerable recurring costs if the system needs constant attention.

Reducing software costs

There are ways in which costs can be reduced. The first applies particularly to bespoke systems and to a lesser extent to modified packages. Discuss the question of copyright with your consultant. If he is originating a package totally on your behalf and you are footing the bill, then copyright should be assigned to you. You may want to discuss the possibility of marketing that copyright, usually by licensing through the consultant. Or you may want to assign the copyright to him in return for a reduced development fee. His attitude to this will depend on the perceived potential market among firms similar to yours and his approach to the whole business of selling, rather than developing packages. Many software developers are seeing the sense of having what in book publishing terms would be described as a 'backlist', to augment one-off consultancy jobs.

I can think of one software firm that has been kept afloat during five years of developing a sophisticated accounts package by the sales of a lowly but effective range of software for home computers.

When it comes to the copyright on modified software, the situation is less clear cut. The original off-the-peg package will probably be under licence and there could be difficulties in actively selling a package predominantly made up of an already licensed product.

Alternatively, you may consider that your package gives you such a march on the competition you wouldn't want it to fall into the hands of anyone else. The trout farm felt just that way about their specially developed feed analysis package and have jealously guarded its copyright. Either way, copyright is a valuable asset; its importance should not be overlooked.

Another way in which you might save money is to join forces with a similar business to arrive at a software package common to both. You may be able to capitalise on work already done by others in your field of business and it would be worth contacting your trade association to see if they know of suitable software/hardware systems already in existence. It should be relatively simple to modify such packages to the individual needs of your business. This is still not a very common approach for reasons of commercial competition but it is worth examining as a possible route to computerisation. The obvious disadvantage lies in the difficulty in finding points of commonality between two business operations. Even if common ground can be found, it may well take more valuable time.

However, there are joint software development ventures, sometimes under the umbrella of a professional body or trade association. The Institute of Chartered Accountants could identify many tasks common to the majority of their members, all of which could be ripe for computerisation. Similarly, an association of retailers could band together to develop software and computer systems suited to their needs. The main stumbling block remains the difficulty of getting agreement on requirements and priorities, and you may conclude that it simply isn't worth the bother just to save a few pounds.

So what could you expect to pay? Well it's unlikely you will get away with less than £2,000 at the very minimum. It is also quite possible, particularly where there is a demand for sophisticated software development or extra hardware in the form of more VDUs, that the bill could run up to more than £100,000. The average business with no fancy requirements could get started on computerisation for under £10,000 including the cost of the hardware. What you do after that is, of course, entirely in your hands.

The hard choice

Once you and your consultant have arrived at a software decision — and remember you are always looking at what the software will do for the business, not what it will do on its own behalf — you will be ready to consider the next phase: the hardware. Such is the complexity of the modern computer scene, it is impossible for one person to know everything about every system. This need not necessarily matter too much for, unlike some of the straight hardware dealers, he or she will not have to be tied to just one machine. Most good consultants maintain a portfolio of the products of at least three hardware manufacturers and are equally at home developing software for any of them. In the main the chief difference between the machines lies in their operating systems. This is the special software that tells the processor how to go about using the main software package. Any consultant should be able to adapt a software package to run on most of the main operating systems.

This brings us to another important point when choosing software/hardware combinations. Hardware and software have to be compatible, but you should also consider future compatibility with an expanded system. Compatibility depends on a number of factors most of them too complex to bother us. Computer language is one. BASIC is well known to many as one of the simplest and easiest for the layman to understand. Others such as FORTRAN and COBOL and PASCAL tend to be found in larger, more complex computers. There are other languages too for more specific computer applications such as Computer Aided Design (CAD).

For many business applications BASIC is being replaced as the most popular programming language so it could be said that the problem of enabling one computer to talk to another is getting worse not better, although compatibility is recognised as a problem which needs to be solved.

Another difficulty lies with the individual operating systems used by hardware manufacturing. An operating system is the means by which a computer sets about processing the instructions you feed into it in accordance with the rules laid down by the software. As with computer languages there are a number; MS/DOS (Microsoft Disk Operating System) and CP/M (Control Program for Microcomputers) are two. Another, rapidly gaining ground is Unix which is said to be particularly suited to business and accounting applications. It's a fast moving area and no businessman can be expected to keep up with all the changes. What he should do, though, is ask his consultant for assurances that the operating system of any piece of proposed hardware will not become obsolete overnight. If you are simply going to bolt on extras to your existing system there should be no problem, but when considering a computer system of higher power a different approach may have to be taken. If you make a quantum leap in computer size, will your existing system with all the data it contains be compatible, or will you simply have to junk it and go through the costly process of feeding all the data in once again?

In case you think this point about the costs of feeding in data is being overstated, let us just consider what is involved. Say a disk holds 500 kilobytes, that's about 65,000 words. (A kilobyte is 1,000 bytes — one byte holds approximately one character of information. Some disks hold less than 500 kilobytes, others far more depending on the system in which they are being used.)

A good typist might get up to speeds of over 80 words a minute, but that is not usually sustainable for any length of time. Let's work on the basis of a typing speed of 65 words a minute, for convenience. Putting in just one disk full of data therefore involves a minimum of 1,000 minutes of typing or 16 hours and that is not the full picture because that figure makes no allowances for errors and corrections and so on. The other point to make is that that figure is only for text. Most computer information in business contains a high proportion of figure work which always takes much longer to input. When we start to take these factors into consideration it is not unreasonable to conclude that the data inputting costs could well run into well over *£100 per disk*! Many businesses will have libraries of several tens of disks. Clearly compatibility is important.

On the face of it this gives the bigger companies with their

So You Think Your Business Needs a Computer?

historical roots in mainframe and mini computers an edge over the smaller firms who supply only micro computers. IBM and ICL are relative newcomers to the small-scale mass market computer, but they have made sure that their new systems are compatible with their larger machines. After all, if you do expand in future, they naturally want to sell you another one of their machines.

Good computer consultants will have an eye to the future and will be able to give you an appraisal on compatibility. They should also be able to ensure that if you plump for one of the smaller hardware firms who tend to offer better value for money in terms of hardware with more 'extras' (such as 'hard disks' for better storage; more 'dedicated' function keys) built in as standard, you will still be able to communicate with larger machines when the time comes.

It is not only the future needs of your own company that ought to be considered, there's the question of compatibility with other outside systems. You may want to tap into databases containing commercial information, or to link directly to the computer of a supplier or customer. These considerations have to be borne in mind before settling on the hardware.

Many consultants will expect you to buy the hardware through them. This is no bad thing: the fact that the consultant will be making money out of supplying the equipment (and margins can be as high as 50 per cent), ought to be reflected in the software development fee he charges you. Additionally, by being the sole supplier of both software and hardware your consultant will have no one but himself to blame when something goes wrong! You can thus avoid the well tried game of shuttlecock, where blame is passed to and forth to the chagrin of the onlooking businessman. Even though you will be putting your trust in your consultant, when it comes to the choice of hardware make sure you involve the staff in the decisions. If you can spare their time let them see the various systems on offer and have the consultant justify his recommendation to them. Even if they are not able to influence the choice of the overall system, they should be allowed an option on the sharp-end elements: keyboards, VDUs and so on.

Training and maintenance

Once the hardware has been specified it is time to look at two other areas. You first need to establish training arrangements for the new system. Who is going to do it? Where will it take place? Which staff should be trained first and so on? Many of these considerations are outlined in Chapter 4 on dealing with the computer salesman. With the consultant you can expect a better response to the whole question of training and also to the question of maintaining the system. In a way the two are interlinked. All too often the system appears to have broken down because of an intrinsic fault in programming when in reality the fault lies with operator error, often due to bad or inadequate training.

It is in the interests of your consultant that your staff become fully versed in the ins and outs of the hardware and its software packages. He will have budgeted a certain amount of time for in-house training and will want to make this effective. The last thing he wants is for him or one of his highly paid programmers to be called back time and again to sort out problems which shouldn't have arisen in the first place. Accordingly, a good consultant will set great store by the training he supplies with the computer package.

Paul Joyce, managing director of Graham Dorian Software of Crowthorne in Berkshire, maintains that training costs for his comprehensive accounts package can add up to almost £1,000 per installation. He, like many other people in the same field, is actively considering the use of video tape to offer long-term training back-up to the initial learning period. This gives the client an easily accessible reference aid when things go wrong, and it gives him more cost-effective use of his staff who are less likely to be called out for problems which, while apparently serious at the time, turn out to be trivial.

When it comes to maintenance, your consultant will first take responsibility for the software. He will probably have an arrangement whereby you pay a maintenance fee — usually 10 per cent a year of the original development costs. This is particularly so with bespoke software. Most developers undertake to deliver it to you 'bug free' to a level of, say, 95 per cent. The debugging process (getting rid of the faults that always seem to crop up when a new computer system is installed), if done properly, involves programmers taking the completed program and deliberately trying to make it crash (stop functioning) by feeding all the kinds of spurious information it might receive simply by virtue of inexpert data inputting.

A good software house can usually cover most eventualities in this way, but there is a law of diminishing returns which dictates that to discover the final 5 per cent of bugs in a program may take an inordinate amount of costly programmers' time. It is usually argued that it is more cost effective to take over the program 95 per cent debugged and stand by to sort out a system crash as and when it occurs. The drawback with this is that your business is to a certain extent exposed to the vagaries of a new program. Not that it happens in every case. The alternative is to go for the final 5 per cent of debugging but this is a costly exercise. Most business people seem to be able to cope with the former course of action.

You should insist that the consultant takes direct responsibility for maintaining the hardware, even if he simply takes out a maintenance contract with the hardware suppliers on your behalf which is then billed to you direct. The main point is that if you are paying for the services of a consultant you should make him earn his corn. Consultants should be able to offer a complete turnkey service (that is a service which is ready to work at the turn of a switch or key), without the need to bother you with the minutiae of running a computer operation.

The long term

We have already established that, if you have chosen your consultant wisely, you will probably want to keep him for a long time. When it comes to computers, there is nothing like continuity, particularly when you have had software specially written or modified for the business.

You should insist that details of the system, both hardware and software, should be properly documented. Any further modifications should be entered into the documentation and updated copies kept on the premises of both the consultant's company and your own. If you want to be particularly sure you might want to consider lodging a copy with your bank for safekeeping. This might sound a little dramatic, but you have to indemnify yourself against your key software man falling under a bus, or the eventuality of your wanting to sack the consultant and bring in someone else. Bringing in a new consultant to fathom out an existing system without documentation is tantamount to asking a child of three to do one of those jigsaw puzzles consisting of thousands of pieces making up a picture when it is predominantly sea and sky.

Very often documentation is overlooked. You must insist that it is accurate, clear and above all, updated every time there is a change or modification to the system, however small.

You may feel that all this is adding up to a lot of money. Well, in computers, as in most other things, you only get what you pay for. Using a consultant is going to cost you more than buying off the peg: more at the outset in capital costs and more in revenue terms with ongoing maintenance fees and modifications. If you have chosen wisely it will be money well spent.

You may, as you see consultancy fees going out month by month, be tempted to try to trim costs by buying in your computer expertise and having it on tap in-house. Some businessmen have tried to tempt if not the principals of software houses, certainly their employees, to join them. This is a mistake, apart from the fact that in real terms, when the long-term costs of employing people full time are taken into consideration, consultancy is still cheaper. The real strength of using consultants is the fact that they should be well placed to pick up on the latest developments in the computer field. If they are doing their job properly they should be able to spot new computer products which could help your business and bring them to your attention. How would someone employed full time by you be able to do that? Cocooned in your business he would simply have to concentrate on your existing system and would be unlikely to bring fresh thinking to bear on your company's computer problems.

In short, when it comes to computer consultancy, don't be tempted to cheesepare on costs. Pay the money and smile in the knowledge that you have used your man management skills to choose wisely.

Case study: Olive Tree Trading Company

Christopher Goodhart is managing director of the Olive Tree Trading Company. Based in Twickenham, they distribute primarily plant containers to garden centres — terracotta, stone, wood, lead and the like from all over the world. They hold a large quantity of stock from a number of sources, all of which has to be sent to myriad destinations.

> The Olive Tree Trading Company was formed in 1979 to import and distribute house and garden products. With rapid expansion over the first four years, it soon became clear that in order to

maintain the rate of growth, and to provide the necessary management information, the company had to computerise.

In early 1984, the busy period (between February and July each year) showed considerable shortfalls in our invoicing and order processing systems, together with major backlogs in the flow of management information. Our first instinct was to approach our accountants and ask for advice. They prepared a lengthy report, recommending two systems based on software operating on the DEC PDP/11 system, which they used themselves. At the time we decided to shelve the project as we felt we could not afford the system, or rather the time involved to incorporate it.

We were approached by a graduate student of the London Business School who wanted to carry out a project for his diploma in management studies. He prepared a very detailed document which suggested that we should spend over £20,000 on an Altos computer, together with a Sun Systems software package costing over £4,000.

After looking at the costs involved and having dipped our toes into the water of computers for some time, we felt that we simply could not justify the expense, and that in any case, to go straight into a fully integrated system would be to invite disaster.

We took a step back and started to look at simpler systems, with off-the-shelf software. At the suggestion of our accountants we had a detailed specification produced and were thus in a position to send this out to a number of dealers.

By this time we had come to the conclusion that there were only three pieces of hardware in the running: Digital, IBM and ACT (Apricot). As far as software was concerned, it became clear that for us the only software package that could begin to give us the kind of integration we required was Pegasus.

Pegasus could give us sales, purchase and nominal ledger, together with stock control and sales invoicing order processing, all fully integrated. This fitted in with our spec, and we found that we could adapt the program to suit our requirements for fine tuning.

As far as the hardware decision was concerned, the answer seemed to be in finding a dealer who could give us the kind of back-up service we required. What this meant in essence was to find someone in whom we had confidence, with whom the chemistry worked. It so happened that it worked with a dealer who specialised in both IBM and Apricot, and we ended up settling for IBM as the larger company with better back-up prospects for the future.

The benefits the system can bring us are in two areas. The first is that we can process our orders with accuracy, advising clients of out-of-stock items when they order, and producing delivery notes and invoices much faster. The second is that we are getting a much more efficient and reliable source of management information for the future expansion and development of the company.

What we have learnt in this process is that one should not be guided by outside reports, which tended to take us towards more expensive systems, but rather follow our own judgement and be cautious and take things slowly. The second lesson was that the hardware is relatively unimportant — given that for our size of company it became clear that we should go for a hard disk machine; whether we chose IBM, Digital or Apricot was a question of empathy with the dealer.

It is not as bad as some experts like to make it seem, but taken slowly and with care, introducing a computer will help us to grow into the late 1980s and early 1990s. Having said that we shall be looking for a new system in two years time!

Chapter 6

Getting Down to Basics

Until now we have dwelt mainly on the philosophical side of introducing computers to business. This is quite reasonable because, unless one gets one's thinking straight, a lot of time and money can be wasted by diving straight in and buying the wrong kind of system, both hardware and software. It is now time to look in a little more depth at what is available to the would-be business computer user. You will realise early on that there is a wide choice. How much of it is of use to the person in business is another matter. Too many hardware and software packages in the past concentrated on achieving momentous feats of intricacy which frequently had little relevance to the real needs of a business operation. This state of affairs has improved enormously but it is as well to be aware of the dangers.

We shall now look at some of the brands of software and hardware now available and assess their usefulness to business, taking aboard some useful background information and tips about the computer world as we proceed. This will not equip you to take on or challenge your computer salesman or consultant, but may help to reduce the number of times you stare blankly at him when he has made a statement about a proposed computer system which, while perfectly straightforward to him, is totally incomprehensible to you.

Because there is so much on the market it would be impossible to consider everything within the scope of this book. What I have done is pick out equipment which, either by market penetration or for design considerations, seems most pertinent to business.

Before we go into detail about individual packages let us consider one or two practical points about software. The first is the form in which the software information is stored.

Storage

Floppy disks

For business use there can really be only one form of storage actively considered, floppy disk. In the main, particularly at the smaller end of the computer market, the industry appears to have standardised on 5¼-inch disks, which is actually the width of the square protective case in which the oxide-coated disk is enclosed. The actual disk diameter is slightly smaller. Disks can be bigger (8 inches) and smaller (around 3 inches).

Disk capacity to store information obviously varies with size, but not directly so. Some disks, given a suitable disk drive, can store information on both sides (*double-sided* disks); others concentrate information so that twice as much can be stored (*double density*). Some even do both, creating *double-sided, double density* disks. Capacity often depends more on the hardware than on the disk itself, but having said that, while you can usually save information on a double-sided disk using a single-sided disk drive, the reverse isn't the case. Typically a 5¼-inch disk will hold 360 kilobytes of information; that's around 150 A4 pages of double spaced typing; an 8-inch disk could hold twice that amount.

The disadvantage of floppy disks is that, by virtue of their very capacity to store large amounts of information in the form of tiny magnetic particles concentrated on a very small and delicate piece of plastic, they are easily damaged. Disks need to be stored in environmentally protected boxes, not left lying around.

Inside the disk drive, the disk floats at great speed past magnetic read/record heads separated by a gap of just a few microns. By comparison, a human hair is six times as thick and could cause untold damage. Even particles of cigarette smoke can cause problems. The ordinary floppy disk has part of its surface exposed to the atmosphere at all times; careless handling of disks can leave harmful fingerprints on the surface.

Some manufacturers have tried to minimise the handling problems by encasing the disk in a far more complicated protective covering; the read/record surface is exposed only when the disk is in the drive and is automatically covered when the disk is withdrawn from the drive. The disk case is constructed from rigid plastic which is far more robust than the traditional paper/flexible plastic materials which gave floppy disks their name.

Although some manufacturers are actively developing this kind of disk, notably Apple with their Mackintosh and Lisa machines and ACT with their range of Apricot hardware, the 5¼-inch floppy will be here for some time, and most software for business applications is available in this format. The widespread use of 5¼-inch floppy disks has caused their price to fall in real terms — it is possible to purchase them for around £2.00 to £3.00 each which is most reasonable when compared with the paper costs alone of storing the equivalent amount of information conventionally.

Microcassettes

There are other storage systems. Microcassettes make use of tiny tape cartridges similar to those designed for storing voice messages dictated into pocket recording machines. These have the same disadvantages of standard cassette drive systems and their application in computers is usually restricted to certain low-powered desk-top machines.

A development of the microcassette is the *microdrive* developed by Sinclair Research. This again uses a tiny ribbon of tape but is designed so that the tape can pass across the magnetic read/record heads at high speed, thus cutting down the loading time. I have used microdrives on the One Per Desk management computer and they certainly seem comparable with disks when it comes to loading and saving information. They have the advantage of being small (each measures approximately 3 × 4 centimetres) and when stored in their individual protective cases they are extremely robust. Disadvantages are their capacity (about 100 kilobytes — a sixth of the size of the average 5¼-inch disk) and concern about the life expectancy of a thin ribbon of tape when it is expected to operate at high speeds. However, with the kind of enterprise one has come to expect of Sir Clive Sinclair, the microdrive loading sequence includes a piece of software that assesses the condition of the tape and gives a read out in terms of life expectancy! That notwithstanding, the use of microdrives does appear to have been limited to a very select range of hardware, notably the OPD from ICL and Sinclair's own range of computers, including their advanced QL machine. I know of no software house that is even considering making its programs available on microdrive.

The cost of a microcassette is relatively high when compared with floppy disks — around £5.00 against £2.00 to £3.00. This is mainly due to the relatively small number of microcassettes in circulation. Nonetheless when you take into account the fact that far less information can be stored on a microcassette they represent a fairly expensive storage and retrieval system.

Read only memory on microchip

This is a system of software storage which holds great promise for the future, namely storing the program in *solid state* on ROM or read only memory. Here all the information is held permanently on microchip, either within the machine or in a cartridge which can be plugged into one of the computer's *ports* (a port is the name given to an electrical socket which enables a computer to be connected to outside devices). With this system there are no mechanical parts — hence the term 'solid state'.

The read only memory means the computer can read and make use of the information stored within the chip but cannot alter or replace it. In this way any software contained in a ROM chip is safe from accidental erasure. However, it also means that the software cannot be adapted or tailored for individual applications. The advantage of this system is that a whole range of programs can be stored permanently in the computer's memory and ready for use as soon as the machine is switched on (this facility can be achieved with a system based on floppy disk input, but only at the added expense of incorporating a *hard disk* — explained on page 149 — into the hardware).

The technique of storing software on ROM has been widely used for computer games but has so far been slow to catch on in the world of business. One reason for this is that such a system is inflexible. But although the program cannot be changed in the microchip itself, it can be altered within the computer processor. The resulting modified program is then stored on floppy disk. Which brings us to the inevitable conclusion that for the foreseeable future at least floppy disk systems of one form or another are going to be an intrinsic part of most business systems. Disk drive systems offer the distinct advantage of speedy program loading.

Documentation

Another factor to consider when choosing software is the documentation that comes with the floppy disk. There is an increasing trend for programs to be *menu driven*, whereby the user simply loads the program and follows instructions displayed on the screen. Each screen display gives the user a range of options. When the user places the *cursor* next to the selected option or simply types out the option on the keyboard, the computer will move into the chosen mode. (The cursor is the flashing square which moves about the screen when the user depresses certain keys. It helps the user to focus on one item of information. Cursor movement is also used in word processing for typing and editing functions.)

Although such systems sound good in theory, I have never yet found a software package where the menus, combined with the *help screens*, are so comprehensive as to render a properly written manual unnecessary. One of the ironies of computers is that while they exist to cut down and ultimately eradicate the need to have information printed on paper, most of the present packages require comprehensive and long instruction manuals if the user is to have any hope of realising the full potential of the package.

Manual

As a computer user you will want to ensure that the manual which accompanies your computer performs many functions.

Training use
First and foremost it should serve as a training document. This section of the manual should contain clear, easy-to-follow tutorials which assume no knowledge on the part of the user (these packages will inevitably need to be used to train staff who have no prior computer knowledge). They should guide him gently through the software. Particularly where complex packages are being used, the training will need to be structured on many levels to take account of the degree of conceptual difficulty presented by the various functions of the software.

Wherever possible, a good manual will teach by example, with specimen cases for the trainee to follow. A really good manual will try to get the user to relate the functions of the software to his own particular business needs, although this is a new trend in writing manuals and there are still very few that make an effort in this direction.

Reference use
The information contained in the training section is then rearranged and collated to form a reference section. This enables the user to look up a particular program function and check out procedures learnt during the training period without having to wade through the whole of the training section. Because in reality different areas of a program tend to be used with greater or less frequency, depending on the needs of an individual business, it helps if the reference section is cross referenced to the

training section so that if a user feels unsure of a procedure he hasn't used for some time he can quickly consult the relevant training example.

Programming
In addition to the training and reference sections, most manuals will have a programming section and one which is usually known as 'Appendices'. The programming is designed to help you, or more probably your consultant, set up special adaptations of the standard program to suit specific applications in your business. It is sometimes known as 'Special applications', whereby you can take the program to the very extent of its abilities and really get your money's worth, should you feel the need.

Programming sections tend to look all Greek to someone who isn't computer minded, but this shouldn't overly concern you as the people who use this section should, in the main, be well used to the jargon. If special applications are designed for use by people unskilled in computers, then they too should be as clearly written as one would expect for the training and reference sections.

Appendices
The appendices of a computer manual contain the vital statistics of the program, usually in tabulated form. These can be of great use in trouble shooting. For example, if a printer refuses to function with a newly installed program, it can often be because the program is not addressing the printer in a way it understands — a problem with the *handshake*. By studying details given in the appendices of the program manual in conjunction with the printer handbook, alterations can be made either to the program or to the circuitry (usually through a series of switches inside the computer or printer) and compatibility established.

As with the programming section, much of the information contained in the appendices will appear impenetrable to the ordinary user. What matters is that the information is there and can be made use of by your consultant or resident expert as the computer system is settled into the business or there is a need to make changes at some later stage.

A good manual should give the impression of having been written by someone who not only knows about his computer but also about the potential user. He should exhibit a sympathy for the difficulties faced by the first-time user. Most important is the inclusion of a comprehensive index. Where possible it should be cross referenced and where a subject appears in both training and reference sections (as most subjects do) then it is helpful if page or paragraph numbers are prefixed with either T or R to indicate the relevant section.

Printed manual documentation, usually in ring-binder, loose-leaf form to facilitate easy updating, may also include other training aids: an audio cassette to be used in conjunction with the manual as with Superbase, a database program from Precision Software. Some software houses are beginning to use video tapes as training aids and the ultimate will come when interactive video disks are introduced. In time they could replace printed manuals completely. That technology is still in its infancy and the origination costs of such material are still too high to be considered for all but the most expensive packages.

The costs

When you purchase a piece of software you are in fact buying the right to use it. Most business software packages contain documentation referring to any licensing agreements which might apply. The idea behind such an arrangement is to protect the software house from unauthorised usage of its programs, and by unauthorised they mean people who have not paid for the privilege. This is not unreasonable as they spend a lot of time creating the program, which is usually their only asset. Software houses are quite naturally jealous of their programs and they protect them assiduously. From the business person's point of view this is a good thing as it establishes some continuity of responsibility in what is still a volatile industry. Most software houses are generous with people who have paid fair and square for their products.

All software houses are alike in stressing the view that what you are paying for is not so much plastic and printed paper as represented by floppy disk and manual, but know-how, brain power, information and therefore power: the fruits of a great deal of time and effort. In a society dominated by the acquisition of material property which you can see and touch, it is sometimes a difficult concept to get over.

The arrangements laid down by the MicroPro Corporation of California are typical of many of the larger business software houses. If you use one of their packages, they relate the number of licences you have to buy (one licence is generally the unit 'cost' of one pack containing disks and manual) to the number of terminals you have in use. One or two terminals require just one licence; three to five, two licences; 10 to 16, four and so on. Should by any chance your business grow so big that you have 100 terminals then MicroPro recognise the time-honoured principle of bulk buying: you will require just 10 licences!

This kind of agreement is not there to exploit a business, simply to ensure a fair return for the software company in direct proportion to the advantage gained by a business using a particular program. The MicroPro arrangement, in common with so many other software houses, does not, for example, prevent you making back-up copies of the program in case the originals are damaged (although many licence agreements restrict the number of copies you may hold at any one time). Some companies even undertake to replace damaged disks free of charge or at nominal fees.

This highlights the importance of registering as a program user with the software house as soon as you acquire one of their packages. It should be looked upon as the start of a long-term relationship which ought to ensure that you are kept up to date with amendments created in the light of the experience of other users, and be informed of new developments and products. Cynics might argue it's just another way of the software houses establishing a mailing list to sell you more of their products, but in my view the new software industry has in the main established an admirable track record in customer relations. Although many companies have been in existence just a few years, most exhibit a pride in their products and a willingness to look at consumer problems that other older industries would do well to emulate.

So how much should you pay? Leaving aside the multiple use of a software package as mentioned in the MicroPro example above, the cost of most packages seems to be geared to cost of the overall hardware system — anything from 10 to 25 per cent. Therefore, if you have a hardware system which cost you, say, £5,000, you could conceivably pay between £500 and £2,500 for a comprehensive software package. This is very much a rule of thumb. It is possible to pay less for the more popular packages, you could pay more for tailor-made or adapted packages.

Another factor is the degree of after-sales service offered by the software house. This is particularly important when considering, for example, payroll software where there are constant updates to take account of changes in taxation laws. In this case you might be asked to subscribe to a software system.

One way of paying less for software is to go for a 'bundle'. Many hardware retailers are 'bundling' software packages together and giving them away at knock-down prices with a hardware purchase. There are bargains to be had but inevitably, while you may get the coveted spreadsheet package, the other software may not be what you wanted. In the end you get what you pay for, but it does pay to shop around.

Chapter 7

Spreadsheets

Different businesses will require their computer to perform a range of different tasks. Let us now look at some of the software on offer at various levels: not a comprehensive tour of the current software market-place, merely a guide to some of the packages available, highlighting some of the points to watch out for when choosing a package for a particular business area.

Using a spreadsheet

We'll start at the low end of the market. Here the hardware is designed to serve an individual manager who feels the need for a computer to help him plan budgets, sales forecasts and the like. The accepted method of doing this is by means of a spreadsheet. The principle of the spreadsheet was around long before the advent of mass market computers and spreadsheets have been prepared in much the same way for over a century. It is simply a way of writing down financial transactions, usually, but not necessarily in relation to time-scale, so as to establish some kind of relationship between the figures. Thus a manager can analyse, almost at a glance, where the money is coming from, and perhaps more importantly, where it is going.

A classic example of spreadsheet analysis is a cash flow projection. Time, as represented, for example, by the months of the coming year is run along the top of the spreadsheet. Listed vertically are the items of income followed by a total figure for all income. Underneath that, expenditure is listed against all the usual headings, heat, light, wages and so on, with another total for overall outgoings. These totals can be compared month by month and the net cash surplus (profit) or net cash requirement (loss) predicted. Monthly totals can be listed separately or cumulatively and the totals can then be carried forward to give a net profit/loss for the year — the bottom line.

So You Think Your Business Needs a Computer?

	October £	November £	December £	January £	February £	March £
INCOME						
Food	7,860	6,540	11,640	6,210	6,850	7,860
Liquor	7,200	5,850	10,350	4,437	6,537	7,200
Total	15,060	12,390	21,990	10,647	13,387	15,060
EXPENDITURE						
Food	2,620	2,180	3,880	2,070	2,283	2,620
Liquor	5,000	5,000	2,000	2,000	1,000	2,000
Total	7,620	7,180	5,880	4,070	3,283	4,620
GROSS PROFIT	7,440	5,210	16,110	6,577	10,104	10,440
Wages	2,000	2,000	2,750	2,000	2,000	2,000
GWEP (gas, water, electricity, phone)	—	—	510	—	—	510
Cleaning and maintenance	350	250	250	750	150	270
Administration and general expenses	235	235	335	235	135	235
Catering supplies	100	200	1,000	500	300	300
Travel and other contingencies	550	500	750	500	500	550
Music, Advertising and PR	—	—	210	—	100	100
Rates	—	—	390	—	—	390
Insurance	2,400	—	—	—	—	—
Bank repayment/interest	500	500	500	500	500	500
VAT	—	—	—	6,200*	—	—
Total	6,135	3,685	6,695	−4,108	3,685	4,855
Balance brought forward	—	1,315	2,840	2,840	8,147	14,566
BALANCE	1,315	2,840	12,255	8,147	14,566	20,151

* adjusted for incoming VAT
Reproduced from *Running Your Own Wine Bar* by Judy Ridgway, published by Kogan Page.

There is nothing very clever about the principle, but it requires a lot of patience to input the figures in the first place, and subsequently to amend them. It also requires a lot of care in carrying out the calculations. Above all, it is time-consuming if done manually; in the past such spreadsheet exercises tended not to be done, except when absolutely necessary (prior to a cap-in-hand trip to the bank, for instance). The advent of computers has changed all that by making spreadsheet analyses simple and available to any business person who wants to use them.

One of the best known is VisiCalc. It was also among the first; others have followed giving greater capacity to handle larger numbers of figures — spreadsheets which, if capable of being laid out physically, would cover several square feet. Other programs reorientate the axes, putting time vertically and expenditure headings across the top of the spreadsheet.

However a spreadsheet is organised, the principle remains the same. Each figure is contained in a *cell* which is given a letter and number just like the square areas outlined on a street map. For example, the cell on the very top left of the spreadsheet will be called A1, as you move the cursor (explained on page 85) over the sheet the cell numbers will change, so a spreadsheet covering 12 months with, say, 10 items of expenditure might well have the bottom-line profit figure at the bottom right-hand corner of the sheet contained in cell N13. You dictate how each cell relates to the others. Some cells will simply hold a figure, others will be the sum of two or more others, or have percentages applied to their figures. The permutations are endless.

Given sufficient capacity it is possible to construct spreadsheets containing many hundreds of cells to take account of various levels of financial modelling within a given business operation. The number of cells you can view at any one time is limited by the video monitor on which you view the spreadsheet. But it is very easy to move about the spreadsheet, using the cursor or special commands which, for example, can take the cursor instantly from top left of the spreadsheet to bottom right. This process is known as *windowing* because in effect you are using the video screen as a moving window which ranges over the spreadsheet.

While it still takes time to set up spreadsheets on computers, once they are there and safely stored they can be used in all manner of ways. Budgeted cash flows can be compared with reality as the figures come in month by month and adjustments are made. Managers can do 'What if?' exercises to see the effects of changing, say, profit margins, or trimming overheads through energy savings, for example. Because it's so much easier to do on a computer, it tends to get done, leading to complaints in some quarters that there is too much theorising and not enough of the real nitty gritty of running a business. There is no doubt, though, that used properly computerised spreadsheets are a real business asset.

Choosing spreadsheet software

Choosing a spreadsheet package should not be too difficult as they are relatively simple pieces of software. What you really should concentrate on when deciding on a spreadsheet package is ease of operation. It should be relatively easy to set up new spreadsheets. Where possible the spreadsheets should contain options whereby you can create standard forms of input. These can usually be amended to take account of any entries particular to your business, but most spreadsheets will require a core of entries that is common to most businesses.

The main differentiating factor between most spreadsheet packages is the size of sheet they can accommodate at any one time. This is a direct function of the size of memory contained in the hardware, so as with other software, any spreadsheet package will have to be purchased with an eye on the hardware you intend using. Large spreadsheets are useful when you want to integrate a lot of information from various sectors of your business and then amalgamate them. This can be done by creating a number of smaller spreadsheets; this can offer greater flexibility, so spreadsheet size should not necessarily be a major consideration.

Apart from spreadsheet size, software packages mainly compete by offering extra facilities such as advanced mathematics which allow you to insert complex formulae into the relationships between the cells; logarithms and linear regression can be included although these functions will have little application in most businesses. If you are planning to use the spreadsheet capability a lot to update information against budgets, for example as the real figures become available, many spreadsheet packages have *automatic form modes* which guide an operator less familiar with the spreadsheet to the various points at which information has to be inserted, reducing the chance of error.

Spreadsheet operation

Spreadsheets are relatively simple to operate, and most people should get the hang of them fairly quickly. As with all software programs, there is no substitute for hands-on experience. This is particularly important if you are expecting to have a number of managers using spreadsheets, information from which may well have to be amalgamated. They should all be using the same system and they need to be trained in such a way that each individual sets out his figures so as not to conflict with another method of input. This is a difficult training consideration, but the process is greatly helped if the software program has facilities for standardisation of spreadsheet layout.

In theory it is possible to build a complete financial model of your whole business operation using spreadsheet analysis. How far you go depends on how much time you are prepared to devote to the exercise. It is doubtful whether completely integrated models can ever really work, because the time taken to gather all the necessary data often renders the resultant information out of date by the time it is available in a form people can understand. Just look at the treasury departments of governments throughout the world with all the computing power they have at their elbows. How many times have they got it wrong? If you restrict the use of spreadsheets to figures directly within your control, with particular emphasis on getting the figures into the computer as quickly as possible, they can be a useful business aid. Over-ambitious use is, in the end, counter-productive.

Other uses

There are other uses for spreadsheets too. You can use them to plan production, updating achievement against targets laid down in a production schedule. Thus it is possible to obtain an idea of how an overall project is progressing and when it is likely to be completed. As more and more real information replaces the estimates and forecasts in the spreadsheet model, the predicted completion date and overall project cost projections become more accurate. You can also use spreadsheets to keep track of equipment and measure maintenance costs. In this way decisions on when to scrap and replace equipment are made easier.

Case study: Bournemouth Business Link

Bournemouth Business Link was set up at the beginning of 1984 to provide a service of secretarial and bookkeeping back-up for small businesses. It was a natural for computerisation and the decision to introduce computers was made that much easier by the fact that the company's founder and managing director, Jeannette Merilion, had spent much of her business career with IBM. Interestingly she looked at quite a few hardware systems before plumping for one of her former employer's products. What is more, the hardware was very clearly of secondary importance to the software in the decision making process.

> To achieve computerisation, we at Business Link first examined very carefully what it was we wanted to computerise. Having decided that we had to decide how much money we could afford before looking at what software was available to achieve what we wanted. In the end we decided on three distinct packages:
>
> 1. Wordstar — word processing
> 2. Pegasus — payroll
> 3. Pegasus — bookkeeping and accountancy
>
> This software was supplied by a local computer dealer together with the promise of back-up to deal with any problems.
>
> Having solved the software problems we set about choosing the hardware. We looked at Sirius. Our business involves providing both accounting and typing services. We found the Sirius keyboard badly laid out for speed when used by a typist, although it was well laid out for accountancy purposes.
>
> Next we looked at Octopus — a computer marketed by TABS software. We disregarded the hardware as we found that the TABS software could not cater for the numerous businesses we were serving. It would have been ideal for one company, but simply was not right for the number of varying companies of differing sizes which make up our client list.

Spreadsheets

We also looked at the Toshiba. We liked the design of the hardware and the software that came with it but found that searching for data was a slow process. Also there was no back-up service available locally.

In the end we decided on an IBM Personal Computer with dual disk drive. To complete the system we bought two printers — a dot matrix for accounts etc, and a daisy wheel for letter quality copy. The choice of the IBM PC was ideal for Business Link as it was supplied by local dealers who provided a 24-hour back-up maintenance service carried out by IBM trained engineers.

Having used the system for over a year we have found advantages and disadvantages. Taking the software first, we find Wordstar fulfils all our word processing needs, although saving (storing on disk) long files is time-consuming. (We have been able to overcome this by limiting the size of files.) The Pegasus payroll package can deal with a wide range of PAYE systems including a complex catering services system. We have to feed Statutory Sick Pay records manually as the software is programmed to summarise employers' and employees' National Insurance. The bookkeeping and accounting package operates satisfactorily, although we find it a little slow because of the way in which the software is programmed to recycle a series of menus so that we have to wait for the computer to offer us a series of options in a precise order before we reach the one we want.

On the hardware side the IBM PC has a very good keyboard, although the fact that there is no reset switch has proved fatal and we have lost a number of files because we have had to switch the machine off and on again to reset it. We also find we need to clean the disk drive heads frequently. The Epson dot matrix printer works well and requires little maintenance. The Brother uses the same daisy wheels as the typewriters we already had — a small saving but a saving nonetheless. Unfortunately the printer is set up for fixed page lengths which causes difficulties when feeding single sheets.

We feel our system has provided us with satisfactory service despite the fact that we had to go computerised on a limited budget. This gave some initial disadvantages but these have now been overcome.

Chapter 8
Word Processing

For many businesses the computer revolution has perhaps made the biggest impact in the field of word processing. Until the advent of computers at a price affordable by virtually all sizes of company, large firms had a distinct advantage over their smaller competitors in all areas where words play a part. It is easy to see just how important the printed word is to most businesses. Everything from advertising through to credit control involves a vast amount of words. Some businesses are conducted solely through mail shots, relying on reams of advertising literature to bring in sales.

Whatever your business, you are likely to benefit from word processing, but only if you have an idea from the outset what the potential benefits could be to your operation.

All word processing packages should give you the facility to create on a visual display screen text laid out in a way which suits you. You should have the facility to edit that text; to insert and delete words, phrases, paragraphs, even whole pages. Your text should be capable of being stored on floppy disks, sent by wire (or even in some cases, cellular radio) to someone else, or be printed out at high speed and sent in conventional fashion through the post.

When choosing a word processing package it is easy to become totally confused by the sheer complexity and sophistication of the software. Such is the competition that the software houses are constantly striving to introduce more and more features to give their products the edge. The result is that because of the time needed to understand all the nuances of a package, the user may take the bit of the package he can easily understand and get into bad habits which only become apparent when another part of the program is uncovered.

What should the package do for you?

The first thing to decide is what you are going to use the

package for. All businesses write letters, so this is an obvious use. But how long will these letters be? Simply one-page reminders to customers who are slow in paying their bills, or circulars and price-lists which you will issue to clients? Virtually all businesses will answer 'yes' to those requirements. Word processing is a godsend for those firms which find themselves constantly having to update a complex, multi-item price-list. In the old days, this would be a lengthy and costly business often involving a totally new origination process: typesetting, proof-reading and reprinting. With word processing you can update a price-list whenever you like. The program will integrate any changes, large or small, and re-create your list in an instant. It can all be done in-house without having to go outside for typesetting, although you may decide to exercise this option as there are still distinct advantages to having certain material printed as we shall discuss later.

Even at this level of word processing, which by computer standards is fairly low, there are certain features you should demand of any package, however basic:

What you see is what you get

This sounds obvious. When you come to print out your information from the screen you should get on paper in hard copy form what you see on the screen. The earlier and more basic word processing packages such as the Commodore Easy Script do not have this facility. Most word processing works on what is known as an 80-column width basis — corresponding to the width of a sheet of A4 paper. Because some packages are designed for use with ordinary television sets which do not show enough detail if the text is condensed to show 80 columns on the screen, only half the page is shown at one time. This is fine when you are using a word processing system to produce page after page of text but it can create difficulties when you want to do something relatively simple like alter the layout of a letter. Fortunately, virtually all of the newer packages designed for business use are for full 80-column display on a high-resolution computer monitor.

Do check that the system does not include blobs, stars or any of the other hieroglyphics that computers often display to indicate that various commands and functions have been entered into the document in question. While it is most useful to have this information it should ideally be displayed separately from the text on the screen in an area usually known as the *status line*. If the information appears in the text itself it can often confuse the operator, although it has to be said that you can get used to anything.

This book was written using Easy Script, which has all the disadvantages of formatting instructions being displayed within the text and a 40-column display. It is a very useful package for simple word processing, although I do miss some of the extra features that are available on more modern word processing programs.

Print and edit simultaneously

This is a must for any business which envisages using word processing as a cornerstone of its operation. If you have a system where the computer is totally tied up while printing out information, then you have a recipe for delay and frustration. Inevitably someone will want to access information while the machine is in printout mode. Not only that, it is clearly wasteful to have an operator skilled in word processing simply monitoring the paper as it spews forth from the printer. Simultaneous print and edit can involve stipulating certain specifications in the hardware, but check first on the word processing package; many of them do not offer the facility.

Fast formatting

Formatting is the word given to the process of turning a piece of text into a predetermined shape or form. The most obvious example of this is an ordinary typed letter.

The conventional format dictates that the address of the sender should be at the top right of the page, the address of the person to whom the letter is being sent on the next line down, but on the left-hand side of the page, the date on the line following but on the right-hand side of the paper under the address of the sender, the text in the middle, and so on. With word processing it would be possible to achieve all of that by simply giving each piece of text a coded label as it is typed in, and then giving the computer a command once the letter is completed to rearrange the text according to a predetermined format. What was once a slab of formless text would in almost an instant be beautifully laid out in letter form. There is really no limit to the way in which formatting can be used, but it scores best where there are complicated formats to be achieved time after time.

A formatting process takes up a lot of computer memory and for it to be used successfully, your word processing package must be able to format quickly to ensure that the word processing operator does not spend valuable time in front of the screen waiting for the computer to perform.

Block ranging

Apart from minor editing, you should also have the facility to move blocks of text around within any given document. You should also be able to save sections of text and drop them into selected documents as they are created. Text should be capable of being moved from one document to another. This is known as *importing* and *exporting*. These functions, like formatting, can take up a lot of computer memory, so not only must your word processing software be up to the mark, your computer must also have sufficient memory to cope.

Bold

With a dot matrix printer (where a series of fine pin-points are impressed on to the paper to make up the character or image) it is possible to obtain quite a range of print effects. The most basic are *underlining* and *bold*, but many packages offer other effects too. *Enhancement* is the facility both to enlarge letters over normal type size and embolden them at the same time. This is very useful for headings and title pages etc.

Some word processing packages also provide a facility for *reversing out* text so that the characters appear printed white on black. Unless you have a very good dot matrix printer this effect is usually unsatisfactory, especially with normal typesize, as it is very difficult to get the background black enough to read the white lettering clearly.

It is wise to check thoroughly the compatibility of the word processing package with any given printer as certain typeface commands can be interpreted differently by different printers. See Chapter 16 for more about printers. It goes almost without saying that should you be using a daisy wheel or thimble printer (where individual pre-cast characters are struck on to the paper, similar to a conventional typewriter) word processing commands will be interpreted differently. With daisy wheel and thimble printer you are limited to using one particular typeface at a time although you should be able to achieve bold and in some cases underlined text.

Additionally most word processing packages incorporate a facility where, given the relevant command, the printing process will pause to allow you to change the wheel or thimble to incorporate different typefaces. If you have a lot of printing to be done, involving many changes of typeface and multiple copies, this is an unsatisfactory arrangement. It is most useful if you want to incorporate a variety of type-styles into a document in order to produce a piece of artwork suitable for photographing and sending to the printers.

The quality of output achieved by dot matrix printers depends on a number of factors. The first and most obvious is price. After that its speed of output. Quite phenomenal speeds can be achieved, running into hundreds of words a minute in some cases, but invariably quality suffers. Some printers offer the facility of slowing down the print speed in order to achieve what is known as near letter quality. This can be enhanced if your word processing software has a *double strike* facility which means that each character is printed twice, each line being printed first on one pass of the dot matrix print head and again on a second pass. The double strike facility can often be used on printers which do not have a capability in themselves of slowing down the print rate. In this way you can make a cheaper printer give more expensive results.

Hunt, search and replace

The *hunt* facility in a word processing package is most useful. It enables you to look through a long document stored on floppy disk and find the section you require without having to read the text from the beginning. Using this facility you might instruct your computer to look for a particular paragraph by number, or by a certain key word. Or you might want to check out all references to a particular subject in the light of new information. Simply key in the subject name and ask your machine to hunt through the text. Each time it comes across the name it will throw up the section of the text on the screen for you to peruse. Once you have satisfied yourself about the first reference you can ask the computer to resume its hunt and it will then find the next reference and so on.

Search and replace is even more useful. With this facility you can go through a text and replace one word with another. For example, you might have written a whole document on fruit importing and referred to bananas throughout the text when in fact you meant to talk about pineapples. Search and replace means you can simply type in the substitute word 'pineapples' once, and the computer will go right through the text throwing out bananas and inserting pineapples.

The same facility can be used to speed up typing by using short forms for much-used phrases. For example, as I am typing this section about word processing I am using the short form 'wp' for word processing. When I finish the text I will instruct the computer to go through the text and wherever it finds 'wp' on its own to replace the letters with word processing written out in full. (It refuses to do a substitution for 'wp' because I have enclosed the letters in quotation marks.)

Search and replace is also invaluable for correcting a wrongly spelt word. You might get right to the end of a document only to find you have consistently misspelt the name of a key customer who may eventually read the finished document. With search and replace you can correct your mistake with little difficulty.

Taken for granted

The five basic options outlined above are additional to the facilities which are these days taken for granted. They should not, however, be underestimated as they provide much more than any conventional typewriter would, but in software terms they are fairly easy to achieve and as such you can expect them in all word processing packages. It is perhaps as well to run through the main standard facilities.

Wordwrap

This is a means by which you can type to the end of a line and not bother to 'carriage return' as you would on a typewriter because the computer recognises that you have run a word over the end of a line and automatically reprints the start of the word on the next line. This facility more than anything else greatly speeds up the typing process, even for the most elementary typists. Most programs do provide a way of bypassing this option, as with long words there are sometimes formatting problems especially where right edge justification is used.

Right edge justification

This is a means by which text is automatically adjusted so that the right-hand edge of the text is lined up straight just like the left-hand edge, giving a more professional look to the finished document. With conventional typewriters you are stuck with a ragged right-hand edge.

Centring

With this facility you can place selected pieces of text in the centre of a line. This most useful facility is far more easily achieved than with a conventional typewriter where calculations usually have to be made to centre, say, a document title.

Pagination

Pages are automatically given a page number as they are printed out, especially useful in long documents. Similarly, with most word processing programs you can make sure there is a *heading* and a *footing* at the top and bottom of each page.

These special facilities, peculiar to word processing, are additional to the functions you would expect to find on an ordinary typewriter, such as margin setting, tabs and so on.

Help!

All these basic word processing functions will be of little use if they are not easy to put into practice. You must make sure that the word processing package you select can be learned and understood easily. There must be a kind of logic about it that will ensure that, especially if you only use a particular function occasionally, you do not have to wade through the manual. Time wasted in this way only serves to negate the purpose of introducing word processing in the first place. It is far better to opt for a word processing package that is menu driven and thus avoid the need to delve into the manual except in dire emergencies. Most modern word processing programs work by requiring a minimum number of keys to be operated for each function. Some of the most frequently used functions, such as *insert* and *delete*, often have single keys dedicated to them.

If all else fails and you get really stuck, a good word processing package will have easy-to-read *help screens* available at all stages in the program to get you out of a jam.

As you can see there is a lot to consider even when you want the most basic of word processing packages. Fortunately word processing is a well-developed area of the software business and virtually all the packages incorporate most of the functions listed above. Once you have considered the basics you are in a position to deliberate on the other facilities you might want.

Spelling it out

If you are planning to produce any large amounts of text for public consumption then you will want to ensure that you get your spelling right. Despite the changing values of modern society, bad spelling can still create a bad impression, whether it be in a simple letter to a customer, a word consistently misspelt throughout a report to a superior, or horror of horrors, in a catalogue or piece of advertising copy. The answer lies in a computerised spelling checker.

Virtually all word processing packages are written so they can be used with a spell checker, although with many of the earlier word processing programs, the spell checkers were often developed later, after the word processing package had been on the market for some time. It is important to understand that a spell checker is not a spelling *corrector*. These rather more sophisticated programs are being developed so that they will not only check but correct spelling as well. While there are one or two such programs on the market, they require so much computer memory that they are unsuitable for the business user.

A spell checker simply works through a piece of text and

highlights words with which it is not familiar. It is then left to the operator to decide whether the word is correctly spelt and to make alterations if necessary. If he is unsure of the spelling he still has to look the word up in the dictionary in the time-honoured old-fashioned way, although some spell checker programs do have a facility whereby alternative spellings can be flashed up for the operator to choose from. Once the operator is satisfied with the highlighted word, he tells the computer (usually by pressing the carriage return key) and the computer continues its search for unfamiliar words and highlights the next one, and so on throughout the document until all the text has been exhausted. It is a relatively simple process but there can be all kinds of operational pitfalls if you end up choosing the wrong kind of spell checker package.

By the time you come to use your spell checker program you or your computer operator will no doubt already have been sitting at the keyboard for some time creating the purple prose which makes up your prized document. The last thing you want to do is spend another period of tedium while the spell checker does its stuff. Sadly some of the earlier spelling checkers took almost as long to operate as it did to write the text in the first place. So the first rule about spell checker packages is that they must be easy to operate. It is still, I am afraid, an all too common practice to sell the spell checker as a bolt-on optional extra to a word processing program; it is a good way for the software houses to collect another fee from the consumer. It is good to see more packages coming on to the market where the word processing and spell checker programs are integrated on one disk. This makes much more sense, as having to load another program whenever you need to run through the spelling of a document is both tedious and time-consuming. So try to find an integrated package; the extra cost will be well worth it.

Another factor to bear in mind is the size of dictionary supplied with the basic software. Spell checker packages work by analysing words in a given text and comparing them with a standard dictionary. Any words which are not in the dictionary are then highlighted for the operator to check. For business usage a minimum dictionary size of 50,000 words should be sought. If this sounds a lot, remember that the unerring logic of a computer counts plurals and tenses of verbs as words in their own right, so you can imagine how easy it is for them to mount up. It should also be possible to add your own words to the dictionary, thus enabling you to customise your spell checker package to suit the specific needs of your business. Most programs allow you to add the specialised words as successive pieces of text are run through the spell checker. In this way you can educate your program to the words unique to your business fairly quickly without needing to input a list of new words.

Most spell checker programs are available in both Standard English and American spellings, but it is as well to check when you purchase the program.

Other facilities available on spell checker programs include *word count*, which is particularly useful to professional writers who make their living by the number of words they sell. It has limited use in normal business applications, but can be useful if word processed text is subsequently to be sent for typesetting, as quite often this is charged for by the word and the spell checker program gives you an independent source of cross reference.

Most programs are also capable of telling you the number of sentences, paragraphs and pages in a given document. Some will also give you an average *word length* which, when you get used to it, is a useful guide to the wordiness or sophistication of a particular piece of writing. Some spell checker programs will also give a *word frequency* report for any given word to check that you are not overworking certain words. Some even highlight commonly overworked words such as 'nice', often with a terse comment to the effect that the word is overworked. Some will also tell you how many unique words, that is words you have used only once, there are in the text.

There are other facilities, but they need not concern the business user. To summarise, the key points to look for in a spell checker package are,

1. Accessibility — the package should be integrated with the word processing software.
2. As large a dictionary as possible.
3. Capacity to add specialised words.
4. Counts for words, sentences, paragraphs and pages.

Chapter 9
Keeping Accounts

Accounts packages are by far the most common form of specialist software used in business. The reason for this is obvious: accounts are usually the most troublesome aspect of running any business, because no one goes into business to run accounts. Most people are in business to sell a particular product or service and it comes very hard to have to buckle down and spend valuable time on generating and maintaining proper accounts. Nonetheless anyone in business who thinks this can be avoided must know the cards are stacked against him, with the VAT man, the income tax people and the bank manager to name but a few, all screaming for tight financial controls. Fortunately this has been well recognised within the software world and there are any number of accounts packages on the market. They are not all the same even though they aim to achieve the same end result. Many vary in their capacity and in their ease of operation. They also differ in their complexity and potential expansion. What you, as the would-be purchaser of an accounts package have to watch out for, is that you can identify within an individual piece of software what it is you want for your business rather than try to fit the capabilities of the software into your operation.

Sales and invoicing

For many people in business, probably their first computer decision is to install a piece of hardware and software to sort out sales and invoicing. At its most basic you want a system whereby the operator can set up for each individual customer a form showing orders as they come in, either by phone or mail, with date of order, date of despatch, date of invoicing, date of payment and so on. This is the first *module* of any accounts package. Within this module you would want the facility to access the accounts to look up information; to amend it; perhaps to print out aspects of the information held on an individual account for use, for example, on a sales visit. You would also want to be able to get reports based on an overview of the module, so that you as a manager could see how things are going. Such reports would perhaps look at a given level of sales over a particular period of time. They could categorise sales by amount — all those over, say, £100 could be listed, or you could list all sales below a specified sum. Frequency of reordering could also be reported upon; what is the average delay between ordering and reordering?

All this information has always been available by analysis of traditional paper-based systems. A computer-based system allows you to access the information with greater facility and speed. Before the advent of computers, such management reporting was never really contemplated in many businesses because it was so time-consuming. For this reason many people in business overlook the reporting aspect of computer-based accounts packages. One of the main benefits of introducing a computer is that it not only helps to streamline the whole process, but also provides much useful management information. So at what stage should a business consider bringing in a computer?

The first thing to note is that the level of sales in money terms is not the main criterion. What really matters is the number of transactions and the complexity of operations. For example, if you are a builder and sell, say, 50 houses a year, the chances are you will not need to computerise your sales and invoicing, as with any luck you should be able to keep track of 50 transactions over a year even though they are each for a considerable sum. (You may well want a computer to keep track of the inputs into your business, but we shall discuss that later when we consider computerised stock control.) If you are running a spare parts business, where your customers can come to you for anything from a couple of nuts and bolts valued in pence to a factory-reconditioned replacement engine valued at several hundred pounds, then putting a suitable package on to the business of keeping track of sales makes obvious sense, even though you may in fact turn over less in a year than our builder who sells 50 houses.

We mentioned earlier the word module. It is vital that we see any sales package as just one part of a potentially far greater accounts software system. Most integrated software systems start off with the order entry/invoicing facility as the base on which the rest of the system is built. Because many accounts packages have been designed in consultation with accountants, they tend to follow traditional accountancy practice with *entries* being *posted* to *sales* and *nominal ledgers*. This is no bad thing, as eventually in any business you will have to answer to the accountant, VAT man, tax man and bank manager, and those are the terms they understand.

Often for relatively little extra cost you can add to the basic sales/invoicing package a sales ledger and nominal ledger. Many software packages come with that facility already built in. To make the nominal ledger side of the software fully effective you will, of course, need to feed in details of purchases. Here things can become a little more complex as some accounts packages deal only with stock purchases. For a fully integrated system which can then go on to supply the full information needed to go to a trial balance and eventually a balance sheet, you need a package which will assimilate details of capital purchases. Such packages quite often are capable of producing an assets register and can also be used for job costing, where complicated calculations need to be done, costing in labour, materials and of course, margin.

Suddenly we have moved a long way from the original problem which usually spurs most businesses to introduce computerisation. You want something that will help you keep track of sales and ordering; something that will print invoices and statements, perhaps even highlight aged debtors. When you take this seemingly simple problem along to your computer software salesman, the tendency is to become bamboozled by all the extra elements of software he wants to sell you. Insist that you look first at the immediate task you want the computer to solve. If it is sales and invoicing then that is what you should ensure you are getting. It is usually relatively simple to add many extras to a basic sales package and not necessarily prohibitively expensive.

Leaving aside talk of ledgers, whether they be sales, purchase or nominal, there is one extra in an accounts software package you should consider at a very early stage in addition to the sales/invoicing facility and that is stock control.

Stock control

Stock control in any manufacturing, wholesaling or retail operation is potentially a bigger worry than keeping track of sales, although the latter assumes more importance because it forms the positive side of cash flow. Stock control is not given much consideration because first, it is tedious to keep tabs on every minute item, and second, to a certain extent losses in a business through bad stock control are easily hidden.

Good software in any business can make a radical contribution to improving efficiency. For if increasing sales can do drastic things to improving the cash flow of a business, just think what tight stock control could do to the other side of the equation. Remember, every £1 saved on the input side through tight stock control can be as effective in improving margins as a £2 increase in outputs through higher sales. With today's accounts software systems it is very easy indeed to link the sales/invoicing software to a stock control package. In this way you should be able to see accurately what your stock levels are at any time you choose, not just after the long and tedious end-of-year stock-take. Not only that, you can see at a glance where your stock is going. If, according to the computer, you have only two widgets left out of an original 10 bought in, and your sales report shows that only six have been invoiced, you will know that two widgets have gone absent without leave. I do not yet know of any software that will actually tell *where* this 'shrinkage' has occurred or indeed *why*, but no doubt there is a software house somewhere that is working on it!

Stock control packages vary in their complexity. Some are geared to sheer capacity, ideal for the business that carries large numbers of stock items (a spare parts business, for example). While this is not a complicated task in itself, it does call for care in the software design so that the computer does not get bogged down while searching through masses of stock entries. Other stock control packages concentrate on the ability to maintain delicate balances between raw material stocks for use, say, in a manufacturing process. This application is of particular value where raw material costs are high and it is imperative to keep stock levels low, yet in keeping with the demands of production. Of course, the stock levels themselves are set by management, often, it has to be said, on a trial and error basis. The computer monitors the situation and sounds the alarm when stocks fall below preset levels. Further sophistication is available whereby levels can be adjusted with one simple command to take account of seasonal or unexpected changes in demand. Some stock control packages even do their own ordering, creating purchase notes or linking

So You Think Your Business Needs a Computer?

directly with suppliers' computers to call up stocks electronically.

We are now a long way away from the simple software of the first-time business computer user. At its most basic, a good stock control package will tighten up your control on stocks and tell you which particular stocks seem to be disappearing. What you do with that information is up to you.

Stay on target

It is very easy to take your eye off the ball when talking accounts software to a computer expert. You have to make sure you introduce a system which will do what you want straightforwardly. It is important not to overlook any potential for effectively developing the use of the computer in your business. So to sum up, when choosing any kind of accounts package the priorities are:

1. Decide what you really want the computer to do — sales invoicing is usually the first requirement.
2. Fully check out how the software works in practice. Ask for hands-on proof (that is, make sure you are allowed to try out the software yourself). Don't be satisfied with merely a demonstration.
3. If satisfied that this is the software for you, find out if other modules can be added to it.
4. Look first for an additional module that will give you stock control.
5. Investigate the capabilities of stock control software.
6. Ask about other modules: sales ledger, purchase ledger, nominal ledger, job costing, production control, assets register.
7. Check on the ease with which extra modules can be installed.
8. Ask about costs but don't be tempted to buy more than you need because of attractive discounts. It will take time to install each module into your business, possibly several months for some. Software costs are coming down all the time and you may be able to pick up extra modules later at a lower cost anyway.
9. Ask about training. How much? Who pays?
10. Ask about back-up and maintenance, should the system crash.

11. Make a judgement about the software company. Are they here to stay?
12. Ask about the hardware. Which will run best with the software on offer?
13. *Make no decision.* Go away, think, consult, discuss for as long as you need.

Many of these considerations can be applied to choosing any software package, particularly the last. Of course, there are other aspects to consider too, like calculating how long it will take to change over to computerised accounts. Increasingly, businesses are not bothering to attempt the transfer of manual records, but simply drawing a line and operating the computer-based system from a given date while running the old system in tandem until the manual system eventually falls obsolete. While this policy can take considerable time, running into years in some cases, it is often the only option open to many companies who find themselves simply unable to spare the staff to do the necessary transfer work. This is particularly true of rapidly expanding businesses who need the computer simply to keep up with their growth.

You will note that hardware is not considered until very near the end of the decision-making process. When it comes to accounts software packages, there is plenty of suitable hardware about, and there should be no difficulty in finding a machine to suit your needs. One or two points need to be considered, however.

Allow for growth

If your business is in a period of growth you will want to estimate and project the number of entries you might make in a working day. Computing capacity is not the problem it used to be and many hardware manufacturers boast that their computers now have 'more memory than you'll ever need'. While that is perhaps slightly overstating the case, it is true that the limiting factor when considering hardware is rapidly becoming not how much memory an individual machine boasts but how quickly the information can be physically typed in on the keyboard. If you anticipate processing several hundred orders a day, you will need more than one terminal. While that is not in itself a problem, it is a factor which has to be considered. Both hardware and software have to be capable of coping with this *multi-user* requirement. Even if you do not anticipate vast numbers of orders occupying the computer system, remember what effects the new-found ease with which you can extract analytical information from the data is bound to have on you and your management colleagues. If you originally bought the system to make it simpler to chase invoices, the time will undoubtedly come when you want to increase the efficiency of your management skills by tapping into that information. Then you will need your very own computer terminal so that at any time you can see how the business is going without having to leave your office. You might not want it now but believe me, it will happen.

Security

Before we leave the subject of access to the information contained within your accounts system, let us pause to consider the significance of what you are introducing. Arguably the accounts are the most important and sensitive part of any business. People can interpret a lot just by looking at them. You will want information to be available only to those who need to know. The trouble with computers is that they are designed to make information easily accessible. Special safeguards have to be built in to guard sensitive information. Most accounts software carries the facility to bar certain sections of the package except to those who have the correct password. Usually these security codes are simple enough to operate while guaranteeing a reasonable level of security, but do check; there is nothing so frustrating as wanting a piece of information and either forgetting or mistyping a complex security code. If you are worried about certain information, for example turnover figures, becoming common knowledge, then make sure that while your staff can put information in, only you can get it out.

Conclusion

I hope you will by now feel that a good accounts package can be a useful investment. Such packages have been around for a long time and in the main the software developers have ironed out most of the early problems. As with database packages, it is probably wise to engage the services of either a consultant or a software house to advise on the package you need. Only by assessing the individual requirement of your business against the range of accounts software currently available will they be able to advise on what is best for you. Whether you are using a consultant or going to a software house, do go through the checklist and satisfy yourself that you are getting what you really need.

When it comes to hardware, the decision is not quite so hard as there is a wide choice. If you are confident that you can accurately measure the potential use of the system you might like to consider using a second-hand computer system, as in the case history cited by Jeremy McLaughlin at the end of Chapter 15. This route can offer considerable savings in both hardware and software. Whether you choose to buy new or second-hand, a good accounts package can, if used correctly, bring big benefits to any business.

Chapter 10
Filing

Filing has traditionally been one of the least understood, and usually the most badly performed of all the office operations. How many top secretaries have had to endure being a filing clerk as the first rung on the office ladder? It is a strange paradox that filing is accorded such low status because it is the bedrock of a company's power and, therefore, success.

Introduction

Filing is, as we all know, a way of storing information. This information may be in the form of letters from clients or prospective customers. There may be price-lists, catalogues (both yours and those of competitors), reports of company meetings, analyses of how changes of legislation affect trading prospects, and so on. It is all information and as such is subject to one overwhelming truth: information is only as good as the ease with which you can get at it!

Everyone in business has probably suffered from the frustrations of needing a piece of information urgently, only to find that it has gone missing. It probably isn't missing at all, simply mislaid. You or your secretary thought it was in one filing cabinet when in fact it had been filed under a different heading. Who is to blame? Well, to a certain extent the system itself.

If you ask your secretary to file a letter, then he or she has only one choice, because there is only one copy of the letter. So it could be filed under the name of the sender (if he is not a regular correspondent, the letter could end up in a general file under the appropriate letter of the alphabet). The letter could be filed under the name of the firm, under a product area or in a file marked 'potential clients' or 'follow up' or any one of a number of headings. Is it any wonder that the letter is nowhere to be found when days, weeks or even months later you call for it. One thing is certain, if you cannot find it when you want it you might as well have thrown it in the waste-paper basket.

So the very system, based on the fact that most letters are still printed on paper, and stored in filing cabinets is to blame. But why not make several copies of the letter and file them under different headings? After all if you judged that the letter ought to be seen by someone else in the company, you will have ordered copies to be circulated immediately. The chances are you would not do that if the letter is merely 'for filing'. Merely 'for filing' is an admission that you don't really know what use the letter is, but rather than throw it away you would rather keep it 'just in case'. Your disdain for the letter is probably communicated to your secretary or filing clerk and as soon as a suitable file is found, in goes the letter and bang shut goes the filing cabinet drawer. Out of sight, out of mind.

The truth is that everything that arrives through the post, even the so-called junk mail, contains some potentially useful information. It might be some time before you can make use of it, but the information is there, even if it is just a name and address followed by brief details. If you were to take a more enlightened approach and ask for several copies of each letter to be made to be filed under various headings, you would be guilty of creating more paper and more work. Computers have the power to change all that!

Enter the database!

A database is the computer name for a very grand filing cabinet which, on top of huge storage capacity, has the ability to sort through vast amounts of data and present it to you in a simple, straightforward way. In software terms it is perhaps one of the most powerful facilities you can have in your computer system. Among the many claims made for database packages, 'power' is the one you will hear most often. The trouble is that while many database packages give you a potential storage capacity equivalent to a whole room full of filing cabinets, they often are not so good at telling you what to put in them or how to set about filling them. Some do not even help you by providing clues in the form of suitable headings for files. The argument for this is to allow you, the client, 'maximum flexibility'.

Using a database requires, more than any other form of software, a readjustment of thinking along logical lines; you really do have to try to think in the same way as the computer. In order to get the most out of a database package it is as well to consider what you can realistically hope to achieve and how to set about it. Let us look at some of the ways in which a database can be applied to typical situations.

Database capacity

Virtually all database software packages offer you the facility of creating as many databases as you want. You can imagine a database to be equivalent to one drawer of a filing cabinet. Within each database there is the facility to store a number of files. The number of files that can be stored within a single database is usually limited. It can be as few as 15, or as many as 100. The capacity of an individual database is tied up with the overall capacity of the computer system. You have to remember that the database is the unit within which the hardware and software sort out and organise your information. This can require quite considerable amounts of computing power and so the number of databases is restricted so that your system does not run out of memory and become confused!

There is no limit to the number of entries you can make in each file except that imposed by the size of your storage system. It must be big enough to store all of one database, so if the database contains more information on file than the capacity of one disk, you will have problems. Careful management of information is needed to ensure you do not clog the system with unnecessary information. Computers operating databases are like human beings using conventional paper-based filing systems when it comes to retrieving information: the more they have to sort through the longer they take to do the job!

Formatting the entries

In each file, within certain limits, you can make as many entries (the equivalent of putting in pieces of typed or printed paper) as you like. To do this you will need to draw up a format. Let us consider one of the simplest.

Suppose you wanted to file all the addresses of your customers. You would devise a form in which you could type in each customer's name and address, line by line. You will certainly want to be able to call up the address quickly and the chances are that when you do this, you will know the customer's name. You want to be able to enter the name into the computer and have the machine find you the address.

Each line on which you enter information in an individual entry is known as a 'field'. A field which you want the computer to be able to recognise as special is known as a 'key' field. With a database package you will have to make sure the customers' names are all entered in areas which have been defined as key fields. Most good database software, but by no means all, allows you to define several key fields in each entry. This can be a double-edged sword, as if the address you are looking for belongs to a customer called Green and you have, for example, an address which contains the word 'green' you may well end up with the wrong entry being displayed. Good database software allows you to differentiate various key fields. You can see that it would be possible to put parts of the address into key fields. If, for example, you specified that the 'city' element (or perhaps a Post Office 'Postcode') of the address be a key field, it would be possible to sort through your clients' addresses and produce a list of everyone coming from a particular city. In theory, it would be possible to sort out customers by street name too although, in practice, it is unlikely that many businesses would want to use this facility.

It is possible to expand the entry to include not only names and addresses but also details of their dealings with you. Every transaction could be listed, in date order. Using the 'numerical field' format facility you can create an entry which would automatically update a customer's account every time you supplied them with goods or services. If they have credit terms, you could also devise a format whereby credit balances were automatically adjusted as payments were made. Additionally it would be possible, using the 'sort' facility of the database, to ask the computer to display all the customers who owed you more than a certain sum. A list of debtors could then be printed out for chasing payment. On some database packages it is possible to sort out debtors by date and even combine date with amount so you can concentrate on chasing up those who have owed you most for longest.

It is not only with customer accounts where databases score. Suppliers too can be put on file in the database. You can ascribe to them various headings under which they might be of use to you. For example, if you had a supplier send you details of his paint and solvent products you could, after entering his name and address, put in fields to cover 'paints' and 'solvents'. You could also add other headings. You could then forget about that supplier until you were in need of, say, paint. Type in 'paint' and the database will sort through and display the names and addresses of all the people who have ever offered to sell you paint. Someone else in your company might want solvents. The same entry will appear when 'solvents' are requested, and so on.

Printed data

One of the most useful facilities of a database is its ability to print out addresses. You can choose who you want to write to, for example all customers who have bought from you in the last year. You can then print the addresses directly on to adhesive labels or, given suitable hardware, on to envelopes, thus cutting out a great deal of time-wasting tedium. By combining the database program with your word processing software, it is possible to write personalised letters to a list of specific customers.

Explore the potential

You are now beginning to see the tremendous potential of databases. They really do offer quite considerable power to any business. The trouble is they are daunting by virtue of that potential power.

You may have noticed that I have not mentioned the database application for that most basic of filing tasks — storing a letter that has been sent in through the mail. Unfortunately this is where databases tend to fall down. For until there is equipment widely available at a reasonable price whereby printed information can be put into a computer by some kind of scanning process, you are stuck with inputting data via a keyboard. This means that, for the time being at least, you will need to specify what information in a letter needs storing and make provision for that information to be accurately input into your computer. You will also need to run a conventional filing system in tandem with your computer database.

What you can achieve, though, with some database software, is a facility whereby a file number is ascribed to a particular piece of print which will be displayed whenever the database throws up relevant data. This cross-referencing of computer entry to hard copy will greatly speed the accessing of filed paperwork without the need to key in every single scrap of information.

For a database to work the whole approach to filing must be elevated above its present level, almost to an art form in fact. You will not be able to avoid introducing a more orderly approach to filing. Staff must be given more training in categorising information; managers must take a greater interest in what they are filing if only to guard their own interests. After all, if you as a manager are more interested in the 'solvents' side of your potential supplier and your secretary chooses to file the information under 'paints' on the grounds that that was the first word to appear, then you have only yourself to blame. Even the best secretaries cannot be expected to be clairvoyant!

What should be clear by now is that while database software can bring big benefits to a business, unlike simple spreadsheets and word processing software, using a database to its ultimate potential requires a real understanding of the logic of computers. The very flexibility offered by the database programmers means a wide range of choices and therefore decisions. You may, as someone who has been involved with business for some time, be able to spot various ways in which a database could be used within your company. Putting your ideas into practice may prove rather more difficult than identifying the problem. So if you are contemplating the introduction of anything more than a simple database for, say, customer addresses, you would be well advised to engage the services of a consultant who can talk through your database requirements, advise on a particular database package and, once it is installed, help set up the formats and systems needed to input and sort the information you need.

Above all, do not allow yourself to be lulled by any advertising claims that a database package is so easy 'a child can use it'. A child probably could, but remember, children are invariably brighter than adults when it comes to computers! Even if you can understand the fundamentals of the package, you will probably not have the time to implement it and get the system you set up through the initial teething period. Your time will be better and more skilfully employed elsewhere within the business.

Chapter 11
Computing the Payroll

An option often considered by business is that of getting the computer to deal with the tedious and often labour-intensive task of working out the wages. On the face of it the computer is the obvious solution to the complex task of sorting out gross pay in relation to hours worked, making deductions for income tax, national insurance and so on, issuing a payslip and keeping a lasting record of pay and deductions for future inspection by business managers and, of course, the Inland Revenue. Quite often weeks will pass with much the same information being repeated on each pay day, so a computer could take a good deal of the drudgery out of the operation. It takes only one employee to fall sick and the whole situation changes. Suddenly the computer is called upon to make calculations with regard to statutory sick pay; other workers may put in overtime to cover for their colleague's absence; the extra hours worked will mean a different rate of PAYE deductions and so on.

All this goes to show that, although there is much tedium in operating a payroll, such is the complexity of the permutations of pay and deductions, the software associated with such a computerised facility has also to be quite complex. The result of all this is that software packages for operating a payroll tend to be quite expensive. Typically you could pay another 25 per cent on top of the original system costs (incorporating hardware and basic software) for a payroll software package. Typical costs for the small-scale computer user are in the range of £400 to £600.

Keeping up to date

There are additional costs too. Apart from training, and a fair deal of familiarisation before a payroll package can be run effectively, there is the cost of maintenance. Payroll is one software package where you simply cannot avoid continuing annual charges, the reason being the ever-changing rules on taxation combined with the fact that employee tax codes are always changing.

As new PAYE tables are issued by the government following a Budget, they have to be incorporated into the existing software system. This is usually achieved by the software house issuing a new disk to its existing customers. Alternatively, some payroll software packages are designed so that they can be 'addressed' by the user, that is you can input the tables yourself without having to wait for a new disk to be delivered. This alternative might appear attractive on the grounds that you are not beholden to the software house for the continuing effectiveness of your software package. Just think what would happen if, for any reason, the software house was unable to deliver the disk until several weeks after the new tables had come into effect!

Most people seem to manage quite well with the kind of arrangement whereby updated disks are sent out as part of the maintenance deal. It is unlikely you will save any money by inputting the information in-house. Typically, a maintenance contract on a payroll software package would cost between £100 and £150 a year which could be money well spent when measured against the costs involved in tying up the time of your own staff. It is, of course, vital to ensure that whoever sells you your software is not likely to disappear and leave you with a software package without back-up.

Running time

Running a payroll package usually takes half a day each time you use it. You might well consider this too long to tie up your computer on a regular basis (remember, you will probably have to run it once a week) arguing that the computer time would be better spent on, for example, processing orders and invoices. Of course, if you invest in a computer with concurrency (that is the ability to run several programs simultaneously), or indeed a number of 'stand alone' machines with a networking capacity, this might not be such a problem. Do not underestimate the computing power you will need to operate a payroll software package which is anything like comprehensive.

The whole purpose of introducing a computer for any

business function is that it will not only perform the task accurately but faster than a manual system. Setting up a payroll package takes as long for a run of five employees as it does for 50. The conventional wisdom seems to be that if a business has fewer than 10 employees, then it is probably not worth putting the payroll on to the computer. Most software houses I have spoken to employing fewer than 10 people do the wages manually.

No doubt sometime in the future there will be more advanced payroll packages coming on to the market. One avenue of research is to link computerised time clocks, including those operating 'flexitime' systems (where employees choose their own hours of work — within limits — and vary them on a day-to-day basis) directly to the computer so that hours worked are automatically calculated and form the basis of weekly or monthly pay summaries. Simple though that may sound in theory, the practice is still some way off except for large businesses with several hundred employees. A scaled down version is likely to come — the question is when?

Summary

When it comes to considering a payroll package, weigh up the following points:

1. Is the business big enough? Fewer than 10 employees — forget it.
2. Can you afford it? The training and the cost of the software itself for a payroll package could cost 25 per cent of the initial cost of your computer hardware. That could be between £400 and £600 for a small computer set-up, much more for larger systems.
3. What about the maintenance costs?
4. Is the software house reputable — will it be around to supply you with updated disks?
5. Can you afford the time to dedicate your computer to running the package — half a day each time you do the wages?

Chapter 12
Graphics

The old saying about a picture being worth a thousand words seems to be increasingly true in business. Time was when people would be happy to be told about future plans. These days it all has to be done with graphs, diagrams and other illustrations backing up words of wisdom. With the computer revolution making it possible to process and analyse more information, more importance is being placed on presenting such information so that it can be quickly and easily assimilated and thereby create the maximum impact. Graphical presentations are much in vogue and because computer technology makes it easier to produce graphics, this trend seems set to continue.

Bar charts

The simplest form of graphics involves displaying a set of figures as horizontal or, more usually vertical columns, called histograms or bar charts. The most obvious example follows on from the spreadsheets created with the help of a financial planning package. Figures for sales can be transposed into a chart on which bars representing, for example, monthly sales can be laid out so it is possible to spot trends at a glance. With many of the more up-to-date graphics packages it is possible to plot other values on top of an existing bar chart. For example, having created a chart for monthly sales over a year it would be possible to overlay figures for cost of sales, again represented as bars. As cost of sales should always be less than the sales figures, the difference between the lengths of the bars in any one month will give, at a glance, a visual representation of the gross profit. The permutations are endless and each business will have its own needs and preferences.

Alternative graphic representations

Some of those factors can be reflected in choosing the right kind of graphics software. Here, as with other types of software, flexibility is the key. You may want to try different forms of graphical representation of your figures — instead of bars, fixed points joined by straight lines, so typical of the classic graphs which seem to adorn the walls of virtually every sales office.

Another very popular form of presentation is the pie chart where figures are represented by segments or slices of a circle. One point here: most graphics systems find it difficult to draw perfect circles so many pie charts look a little ragged at the edges. Nonetheless this presentation form is particularly useful for the analysis of expenditure — you can actually see who is getting the biggest slice of the cake.

Most packages offer the facility of different representational forms, but do check that you can alter and move the figures about once they have been input. Some packages developed in the early stages of microcomputing insist you opt for a particular style of graphical representation before you input figures, thus denying you the possibility of changing your mind about the graphics style later on. Do make sure that the graphics package you buy does not hem you in like this.

One of the real boons of recent software development is the ability to *import* information from, say, a spreadsheet and have it instantly translated into graphs. This development is bound to continue as it seems that designers of both computer hardware and software have at last grasped the point that most businesses simply do not have the time to fiddle about making the computer work; they just want it to get on with the job in hand.

Software packages

Some of the graphics software packages available are still too sophisticated for everyday use in real business environments. They often require a high level of training before the operator is able to achieve a reasonable facility with the package. Unless the business has a constant demand for the graphics produced by the package it is unlikely to be worth the investment in time and money.

Some packages are quite the reverse: they are so simple as to be of no use at all, usually because while they can probably create the pretty pictures, they do not have the extra facilities which enable figures to be imported from other files and then adjusted and moved about at will.

Colour

Each business will have to assess its own needs, but it is important not to be taken in by unnecessary facilities which may mask the fact that other far more useful functions are simply not available. Take, for example, the business of colour. Many programs boast the ability to produce colour graphics, but for average business use this is a luxury which, while not necessarily expensive in terms of the package itself, can start costs spiralling if you try to make the same use of colour graphics as you would of graphics in monochrome. The reason for this is quite simple.

Any good dot matrix printer should be able to create an acceptable screen printout of a graphics display, but if you want to reproduce the colours on the screen it's a different matter entirely. Colour printers are not only expensive, they are slow, and there are very few which give an adequate representation on the colour computer screen. True, there are some which have facilities to draw in colour the large transparent slides or cells used for overhead projectors, but such printers can cost almost as much as a good micro computer itself.

While colour graphics may look good on the screen, if you want to show the same display to someone else by sending it in hard copy form through the post, then it is going to cost you. In the main people are usually able to make do with a black and white copy anyway, so why not just settle for a black and white graphics package in the first place? In any event, do not allow yourself to be hoodwinked by the hype that so often builds itself around the wonders of 'colour graphics'.

Sharpening up the image

Watch out too for talk of *pixels* and *sprites*. A pixel is the name given to the smallest block of light that can be projected on to the VDU screen in any given system. The more pixels per square centimetre the better the image. A good comparison is the dots which make up a newspaper image; the denser the dots, the better the definition of the picture. A sprite is an area of the screen comprising several pixels which can be altered in colour or intensity and also moved about the screen. Most business users of computers can safely forget about them. In the main you need only worry about sprites and pixels if you are planning to write your own software for computer arcade games; it is unlikely you will need to be concerned with them if all you want is a good workaday graphics package.

Summary

'Workaday' is the key word when choosing graphics packages. You have to arrive at a compromise between the sophistication so complex as to require a long period of training and constant use by an operator to become familiar with the program, and a program too simple to meet your requirements. If all you think you will need is a package that will create graphs which can subsequently be easily printed out in black and white, then go for a simple (and probably much cheaper) package, but make sure it has the capability of handling figures in such a way that leaves you the option to change your mind.

Chapter 13
Getting the Message

The third stage of word processing takes you that last vital step towards a truly paper-free office, but the computer revolution makes so much more information available at the touch of a few buttons that the demand for this information in printed form is bound to mean more paper around the office not less, for the time being at least. Even so, there are now real signs that we are beginning to move slowly towards the promised dream. This all comes about because of the advent of messaging which, quite simply, is computerese for the ability to send sections of text, and now in many cases, data, in graphical form, to another computer. In theory, that computer could be thousands of miles away on the other side of the world. All that matters is that messages can pass between them, usually down a telephone line. In practice, most businesses need computers to be able to talk to each other on three levels of priority.

1. Within the company.
2. With customers and suppliers within the home country (usually the main market).
3. With company branches, customers and suppliers abroad.

Whichever option applies to you, choices of messaging systems tend to narrow at this point. It is still very much a question of selecting hardware and software together, as there is little room for mixing different systems at the moment. We shall be discussing hardware in more detail later but as the most likely form of data you will want to 'message' will be words, it seems sensible to consider the messaging options here.

Messages within the company

Looking at option 1, it seems likely you will want to use messaging to ensure that information is shared among those who need to know. In theory, this is a praiseworthy ambition and one which should be pursued, as all too often businesses have come near to foundering because not enough people were 'in the know' at the right time. 'A problem shared is a problem halved' and anything that gives the widest number of people the opportunity to share that problem and come up with suggestions for a solution, the better. Using messaging to overcome this difficulty will require a radical change in the working practices of your management team and you should not expect these changes to come about overnight. Used correctly, the potential management benefits offered by an efficient messaging system are enormous, some would say even frightening.

Additionally, a member of management would be given a task and a time in which to provide a solution which would then be presented, usually at a meeting of his boss and his peers. Messaging gives you the facility to check the progress of the 'task solving' at any stage. Through the wonders of word processing it should be possible for senior management to demand that interim reports on the state of play be sent regularly. Old excuses based on the shortage of typing time should be a thing of the past. Shrewd managers will probably reason that the best policy is still to let a subordinate 'get on with the job' once it is set. No computerisation should be used as a blunt instrument with which to instil fear.

The real advantage of messaging lies in the potential for sharing information, for while messaging is normally thought of as a system for sending information out, it can, of course, be used equally efficiently for getting information in. In a traditional paper-based office, information usually exists only in a single copy stored away in a filing cabinet. The sheer bulk of paper filing systems makes it difficult for large amounts of duplicated information to be kept. And even when this is considered a necessity and long-term copies are made, perhaps on microfilm, someone has to decide which information should be kept and this in itself requires yet more management and staff time tied up doing the work. With a computer-based information system it's different.

Because the information is stored and accessed electronically, several people can use the same information at the same time. The effect on efficiency of 'multiple access' can be quite marked. No longer will the excuse, 'Someone else is using the file' be valid. This facility can, in theory at least, provide some mischief for the employer. He could, independently, set two of his staff the same problem and see who came up with the best solution first in the sure knowledge that they both had access to the same information. What is more, neither need necessarily have known that someone else had been set the same task.

Option 1, messaging within the company, provides the greatest opportunity for shared access to information. Here you can ensure that everyone is using the same type of equipment which, by definition, will be able to 'talk' the same computer language. Many of the larger computer manufacturers are offering what they call 'cluster packages', whereby with the addition of some extra software, several of their traditional 'stand-alone' machines (machines which are totally self-contained and need not be connected to any other computer to operate) are joined together and connected, usually through 'dedicated' wires. Sometimes extra hardware is incorporated, especially where a real need for shared information is identified. Usually such systems will be installed on a customised or semi-customised basis. For the manufacturer, it is an obvious way of selling more hardware, and as prices continue to tumble, pressure to sell more units intensifies.

One manufacturer, with a history which stretches back to the first days of mechanical typewriters took the decision in 1985 to leave sales of stand-alone machines to its appointed dealer network. Its own directly employed salesmen were to concentrate solely on selling clusters, thus making their selling time more effective.

While most of the semi-customised cluster systems offered by the big manufacturers may well be perfectly adequate for most business needs, if you feel there is a real need for people within your company to share computer information either by having access to the same data or having the facility to pass around information (for example management reports), it is worth looking at some of the systems which have been specifically developed to achieve this.

Information Technology Limited are now actively marketing a system known as IMP, which stands for the Information Management Processor. Here, single work stations (a work station is the name given to a terminal which normally relies on being connected to a larger computer to function), usually one on every manager's desk, are linked through a central controller. The work stations can function quite happily on their own, carrying out all the normal business computer functions, word processing, financial planning, graphics and so on, but at any stage the user can send information through the central controller to another work station within the system.

The central controller can store documents electronically. A work station can access this information at a later date. The same information can be accessed many times by several work stations, so that no one need be held up by the fact that a file is 'out'. The central controller, although only about the same physical size of a two-drawer filing cabinet, has vast storage capacity. It will hold not only files but also messages. For example, if a message is sent to someone who is not at his work station, the controller will hold it until he returns. A message can be anything from a short two- or three-line memo to a report of several pages.

Where the IMP really scores is in its ability to receive and hold voice messages. Most business communication still uses speech for the simple reason it is the most accessible and versatile communication medium. By integrating voice communication, the IMP has taken high-speed business communication another step towards what I suppose must be the ultimate, thought communication. Happily that particular facility is still some way from becoming reality.

Introducing a system such as the IMP calls for a deal of planning. Who will need a work station? Although the central controller can hold all files, some, personnel files for example, may not be for 'all eyes'. It is possible for files to be restricted by ascribing access codes to them but again, a hierarchy has to be worked out. Again more planning. Systems such as the IMP require their own special wires to link them together. Unless your existing building has already installed suitable cabling, then you can expect more upheaval.

Distance messaging

Another messaging route is that pioneered by ICL. They were the first to bring out a cheap, no-nonsense work station which provided an easy messaging system through existing telephone lines. They called it OPD, an acronym for One Per Desk — a clear indication of how many they intended to sell. Here, messaging is not restricted to the company, country or even the world, although to talk directly to another computer user, you would have to make sure that he had another OPD. In an attempt to improve this situation, from the start ICL enabled its OPDs to link into some of the proprietary messaging systems: the British Telecom 'Gold' system, for example. OPDs can also link into commercial databases such as Prestel, again through a telephone line.

What OPDs cannot do is share applications software. Given that virtually all the software needed for everyday use as a work station is built in on silicon chip, that is not a disadvantage necessarily. Because there is no central controller, the OPD system cannot store messages. They can only be sent to other OPDs if those machines are switched on and working, although if you leave your desk you can program your own work station to answer the phone for you and announce a message to the effect that you are not there, albeit in a robotic sounding, synthesised voice.

Messaging offers great opportunities for vastly improving the efficiency of any business operation where a lot of information has to be transmitted to a number of key people quickly. If several people need to access, comment upon and amend documents, then some kind of messaging system is essential.

The difficulties lie in problems of compatibility between systems and the fact that no one system at the moment looks like dominating this particular section of the market and thereby setting some kind of common standard for others to follow. There are signs that smaller hardware manufacturers are coming on to the scene, and, like the cottage industry software developers, producing solutions. Already there is available a range of 'smart cables' which, through built-in circuitry at either end of the wire, help to sort out the incompatibilities between different pieces of hardware and allow them to work harmoniously together. So far, smart cables have been chiefly of use in enabling a wide range of printers to be hooked up to a variety of computer systems.

No doubt similar devices will become available to enable messaging between different hardware/software systems. When such devices do come on to the market there will inevitably be a price to pay. Typically, smart cables for printers cost more than three times the price of ordinary cables. 'Smart' systems for messaging will have to be more complex and they will cost commensurately more.

For the moment you are faced with the choice of going for a unified system which will mean taking on board one single manufacturer and probably a limited range of software, or using the public messaging systems through the telephone network. On balance the latter is probably the better bet as it offers flexibility in computing software, combined with the facility to tap into other computers when you need to.

Costs

If you decide that you want to put computing power into the hands of individuals within your business operation and have them share and pass around information, then systems such as the ITL IMP or the ICL OPD are worth looking at. With costs of individual work stations ranging from £1,300 to £2,500 each you will have to decide if you can afford to give everyone a computer. If you cannot afford a computer on every desk you will have to draw up a priority list. There is a strong argument that if there are not enough work stations from the start you will defeat the object of the exercise. Much will depend on your assessment of how much real benefit they can bring to your business. It is unlikely, though, that individual desk-top computers will also be the right answer to the principal computing problems of your business.

Chapter 14

Software — the Next Step

So far we have covered the types of software which are generally considered essential to all businesses. With packages for spreadsheet analysis, word processing, databases and graphics, most businesses should be able to benefit from computerisation.

It is now being recognised by both hardware and software manufacturers that a very large section of business will have no need for much more than these four basic capabilities plus a messaging capability, and increasingly we find hardware being offered complete with 'bundles' of software that will achieve the major computing functions. This policy makes it relatively simple to ensure that all your software is fully integrated so that, for example, while writing a report using the word processing package, you can incorporate figures gleaned from your spreadsheet and subsequently display them in graphical form, finally printing out the whole document with no worries that a particular piece of software will gum up the works. Having achieved that, you can go on to personalise the document and finally send it out to a list of customers using addresses stored in another part of your database. Ultimately, all of this could be achieved by electronic messaging, without a single piece of paper being printed, though until electronic messaging becomes much more widespread it is likely we shall still need to generate paper in vast amounts.

This describes what the computer industry would like to be the way forward. However, computer systems which achieve this rounded approach are seldom the complete answer to most business needs. The reason lies in the fact that every business will have differing needs. To satisfy their requirements most businesses need to look at specialist software packages. Space does not permit us to describe every type of specialist software on the market.

Specialist packages

If you are interested in such packages, the rules for choosing them are much the same as for the more generalised software. They are summarised in the following checklist.

1. Make sure the software fits in with your business operation — not the other way around.
2. Count the costs both of purchase and maintenance.
3. Calculate the effect of the new software in terms of computer time. How will it fit in with other software?
4. How easy will it be for your staff to get the hang of the software? If you have a complex, hard-to-learn package with whistles and bells, it will have to really benefit the business to justify the time staff take to learn how to use it.
5. Will the software package really do the job more quickly and efficiently than existing methods?

Now you have come this far, the really hard bit is over. You should by now have a fair idea of what you want out of your software. The next step, choosing the hardware, is relatively easy. In the following chapter we shall look at the hardware options and see how to maximise the effectiveness of a computer in your business by adding wise choices in hardware to smart software choices.

Case study: RJL Software

RJL Software was founded in 1982 by Richard Lamb. A trained programmer, he wanted to provide a bespoke computer service for business clients, particularly those companies for whom an off-the-peg package was not the entire answer to their computer needs. Among the clients served from his Winchester-based office was a trout farm which needed a complex program to record the frequency and the amounts of feed given to thousands of fish of differing sizes. At the other end of the scale, RJL Software also offers comprehensive back-up to users of standard software packages. Richard Lamb's broad experience gives a useful insight into how a computer professional regards the would-be business user.

> In our experience there are three types of computer user: those who do not wish to spend any more money than they have to,

those who expect something for nothing, and those who expect miracles!

Our first experience of those who do not spend any more than they have to was when we lost a sale to a computer retail outlet — more often known as a 'chip shop'. We spent several hours talking to the potential client. We advised him and gave him a demonstration of the type of software that we felt would best suit his requirements. Several days later our potential client telephoned to say that he had considered our proposal but had also seen the same hardware demonstrated at a reputable local computer retailer and it was 10 per cent cheaper than our price. The client had also been promised similar software packages to those proposed by ourselves. We explained to our potential client that our prices included training, installation and a full back-up service but he still decided not to purchase from us. Within two months we had a call from him. He had had his computer for six weeks and it still did not work. Could we help him?

From an inspection of his software it was obvious that it was a pirate version, hence the big difference in price compared to the package we had offered him. It was also obvious that the local reputable computer retailer did not understand the products he was selling. Not only had he sold the wrong operating system, but he had also supplied the wrong interface cable for the printer, thus ensuring that the computer system would not work.

One of our experiences of the type of client who wanted something for nothing came shortly after we had installed his system and fully trained his staff. The system we had supplied was very flexible and enabled the user to design his own reports. Prior to the sale we agreed that three days would be spent on installation and training. Within six weeks of installation the client was so impressed with the speed and flexibility of the system that he started to design his own reports. Unfortunately he did not fully understand the report designer system and had to call us in to correct his mistakes. This necessitated a 100-mile round trip and a day out of the office for one of our programmers. Our invoice to the client was just £50, merely to cover the overhead of the member of staff concerned. It was two months before this invoice was paid.

A third example, someone expecting miracles, concerned a potential client to whom we were recommended. When we met the client he informed us that he wished to use his son's home computer to compile the accounts for his business. We explained that this was possible if he was prepared to add a disk drive and printer to his current system. This we told him would cost in the region of £500. We also explained he would need additional software costing around £300. We were quickly shown the door! Our potential client was only prepared to spend £300 to run a full accounting package using a cassette tape player and a dot matrix printer.

These examples are just a small demonstration of how many people looking for a business computer system simply do not understand that the most important requirement is proven software from a reliable supplier with full back-up and service support and the potential of growth within the system chosen.

Chapter 15

The Hardware

Hardware is the name applied to any part of a computer system which is, quite literally, 'hard'; it is, if you like, the 'boxes' which contain the electronics which make a computer function. The whole computer industry has been dominated by the big manufacturers of hardware: IBM, Apple, Commodore, ACT, ICL and so on.

When computers were first invented they were virtually all *mainframes*, that is large machines often filling a whole room with equipment, with an array of energy-consuming electrical valves which formed the basis of the system. Valves soon gave way to transistors, the invention of which took computers on the first leg of the trip towards miniaturisation, giving more computing power in a smaller space. For this smaller type of computer the name *mini* was coined.

The real revolution in computer technology came about in the sixties with the invention of the silicon chip. With the chip came the potential of putting hundreds of transistors on just one tiny sliver of semi-conducting material; Pandora's box was now fully open. Such capacity for miniaturisation led the way to the invention of the *micro* computer. Today the lines between mainframe, mini and micro are somewhat blurred, but when people now refer to a mainframe they probably have in mind the computing capacity approaching that of the huge CRAY computer installations (the largest computer in the world which numbers among its applications complex scientific calculations designed to unlock the secrets of the universe) paid for in multi-million dollar deals, and only affordable by the really enormous multi-national companies or governmental institutions such as the Pentagon.

Micro computers

Mini computers are within the reach of most large businesses, but the real democratisation of hardware has come with the advent of the micro which is so priced as to be within the reach of virtually every school and college, and certainly within reach of all businesses. It is outside the scope of this book to discuss anything other than micro computing systems. Without an understanding of what micro computers can offer, it is unlikely you would be able to make much sense of larger installations.

The hardware of a micro computer consists of the *central processor, keyboard, visual display unit* and the *peripherals*, such as *printer* and *disk drives*. Of these by far the most important is the central processor; the others are then selected to fit in with it.

The central processor

In essence the central processor is the 'brain' of the computer system. This is where the computer does its 'thinking'. The information is altered, analysed and sorted.

Capacity

The key factor in choosing a central processor is capacity which is the amount of work the central processor can take on and process at any one time. This is usually measured in *kilobytes*, that is thousands of *bytes*. A byte is a term invented by computer people. Each letter or character requires one byte. It is obvious that a kilobyte does not represent much capacity.

The capacity of the central processor on a business computer can range from 64 kilobytes upwards. A central processor requires capacity for two reasons. One is to deal with the information you put into it, but before it can do that it must already have the ability to deal with that information. It does this by using a combination of an operating system — the basic ABC of computing which tells the central processor how to run itself — and of course the software, which tells it specifically how to process information. Both the operating system and the software take up space or kilobytes within the system. If there is a finite capacity, space taken up by the operating system and software will leave less for dealing with information. The more complicated the software, the more capacity will be required in the central processor.

With smarter and smarter chips becoming increasingly available, central processor capacity is going up all the time. It

The Hardware

is now quite easy and relatively inexpensive to have central processor units with capacities of 256 kilobytes, 512 kilobytes or even more. You cannot have too much capacity and this is recognised by some of the more enlightened companies such as Apple, who advertise their computers with 'more capacity than you'll ever need'.

It needs to be stressed that the available capacity for information processing is what matters. Some operating system software takes up much more space than others; it's the same with applications software too. Some of this can be overcome by 'building in' the operating system (and in some cases software too) so that it is permanently available on chip. This is known as ROM capacity. ROM stands for Read Only Memory and, as its name implies, it is information that can be read by the central processor but not altered. ROM is only as good as the information that it contains.

RAM stands for Random Access Memory. Information on RAM can not only be accessed but it can also be altered, sorted and erased. RAM is what matters when deciding on central processor capacity. You will need to know how much of your information the central processor can deal with at any one time, so if the operating system and the software take up a certain amount of the capacity available on RAM, check what the usable RAM capacity will be.

Many businesses can get by with systems containing quite small central processors and capacity will depend very much on the use you make of your computer. To be safe you should be looking for over 100 kilobytes of usable RAM, but you may well need much more, particularly if you are planning to use some of the more sophisticated software packages.

Concurrency

Another function a business user should seriously consider is concurrency. Concurrency is the ability of a computer system to be able to run several software programs at the same time. This applies mainly to the larger micros, but increasingly as the technology advances it is becoming available at the lower end of the business market.

At its most basic, concurrency allows you to print out a document from a file while working on another document. Many micros totally tie up the central processor during the printing process, creating expensive time-wasting delays in the **operation of the business.**

The next stage up the concurrency ladder enables you to run, say, four and then eight different programs simultaneously and import and export information between them. So you could, for example, bring in a graphic display to be included in a document being prepared using the word processing software. The central processor alone is not enough to determine concurrency; it has to have the right operating system. In practice this probably means that you will be funnelled down one particular road when it comes to choosing suitable software to run concurrently. You may consider this narrowing of options a disadvantage.

Expandability

The third consideration when choosing the central processor is expandability. Virtually everyone who buys a computer ends up wanting it to do more and more. It is as well, then, to ensure that you can increase the capacity of the central processor. The alternative would be expensive. Not only would you have to consider throwing your existing system away, you may find the new, larger system incompatible with your existing software and, in all probability, with the disk-based information you have built up in the time you were using the smaller system.

The first difficulty can be resolved by checking with the hardware salesman about the availability of extra capacity. IBM micros, for example, are designed so that you simply add an extra circuit board or two to increase the range of the machine. Other hardware manufacturers offer the same facility. (When the Symphony package of integrated software was launched, many users discovered that not only did they have to shell out over £500 for the software, they also had to upgrade their existing machines so that the central processor could run the program.)

If your business expands greatly there will come a point when you just cannot cram any more boards in. For other reasons too you may want to go for a completely different set-up. This is one of the strongest reasons for opting for a micro produced by one of the larger manufacturers. If you buy a micro at the bottom of a large range of computers which extends right up the scale, it is obviously going to be easier to move up to, say, a mini than trying to upgrade a one-off model produced by one of the small scale manufacturers. In most cases you would have to discard the smaller machine and start again. Where small manufacturers usually score is that their machines generally offer more computing power for the price.

The choice will be either paying over the odds for a micro produced by a large hardware manufacturer or getting a machine that is better value for money and taking a risk of incompatibility at a later stage. The latter possibility might become less crucial as the technology develops. Already there are signs of work being done to produce, in the absence of any real industry standards, equipment which will enable computers using different operating systems and software to talk to each other.

To sum up, when it comes to choosing a central processor, you will need to be assured of the following:

1. *Capacity*. You should be looking for usable RAM (that is RAM not taken up with running the operating system of the computer) of over 100 kilobytes.
2. *Concurrency*. Will you want to run several programs at the same time? If so check that the central processor can cope with this.
3. *Expandability*. Is the central processor capable of growing with your business? Check too that you can move up to larger computer products from the hardware manufacturer's range with ease and economy.

Keyboards

Keyboards are the means by which most information is put into the central processor for processing. The choice of keyboard will depend largely on your choice of central processor. Generally speaking, they come together. However, given that you have narrowed down your choices of central processor, you may well find the keyboard will sway your decision.

The keyboard will consist of a set of typewriter keys with the standard QWERTY layout. The QWERTY layout was originally designed for manual typewriters, and was based on the need to ensure that letters which frequently followed each other would not jam during high speed typing. Such is the universality of the layout it has been adopted for computer keyboards although, as there are no mechanical parts to worry about another, more logical layout could have been adopted.

In addition to letters and punctuation there will be other keys designed to help with the various functions of the computer. The numbers and types of these keys vary according to what the computer is expected to do. For specialised usages there will be specialised keys. More generally, computer keyboards tend to separate out specific function keys, either horizontally in an extra row, or to one side of the keyboard.

Additionally there may be a separate *number pad* for swift entry of figures. If you envisage your computer being used for accounts, payroll etc, a number pad is essential. Do check that, in addition to the numbers themselves, the various function signs for adding, subtracting and so on are grouped within the number pad. One keyboard I came across had the numbers in one place, together with the addition and multiplication signs, but expected you to go back to using shift keys in the main QWERTY pad for subtraction, division, percentages and equals — very irritating.

To offer as many functions as possible most computer keyboards have extra shift keys, usually marked CONTROL or ALT (for 'alternative'). It is as well to check how these are positioned; often they are too close to the main QWERTY layout and accidentally hitting one of them can cause disastrous results.

The other factors to consider when choosing a keyboard are mainly ergonomic. For this reason it makes good sense to get the opinion of people who are to use the keyboard. They will have their own preferences for keyboard 'feel'. Inevitably these will vary from person to person, but even those used to electric typewriters will, after a relatively short time, appreciate the ease with which a computer keyboard can be used. They will have views too on other factors, such as the rake of the keyboard. Some can be adjusted, others are fixed. Most keyboards these days are light and portable, connected to the central processing unit by a flexible lead. This allows people to use keyboards on their laps if they wish — a practice which can help to reduce operator fatigue.

An alternative to the QWERTY keyboard exists in the form of the *Maltron* keyboard. This consists of a tiny unit with literally a handful of buttons, operated by just one hand. By pressing the buttons in various simultaneous sequences very fast word inputting speeds can be achieved. This device, called the MicroWriter, has carved a fair niche for itself as a highly portable memo writing machine whereby documents can be

The Hardware

typed silently on trains and aircraft. With the advent of portable computers with up to eight lines of 80-character display and a full size QWERTY keyboard, it is doubtful whether the Maltron device will maintain its position. Such is the hold of QWERTY-based keyboard training it seems unlikely that Maltron will ever gain a real foothold in an office environment.

The mouse

There are alternatives to keyboards, the mouse for example. This is a device in the form of a small rectangular box connected by a lead (it looks like a tail, hence the name) to the central processor. By moving the mouse about a small area of desk space you can control a pointer displayed on the screen. By pointing, for example, at various pieces of text you can move them about for editing purposes and so on. The mouse system has been developed largely by the Apple Corporation and it is widely used on their Mackintosh range of micros. Functions are displayed pictorially in the form of *icons*. So if, for example, you want to scrap a piece of information, instead of typing 'delete', 'erase' or 'scratch' you use the mouse to position the pointer over a picture of a waste-paper basket. The idea behind the mouse is to overcome keyboard phobia, but remember it really is limited to altering and amending information already within the system. Inputting original material still has to be done via a keyboard.

Touchscreen

It's the same too for the touchscreen system. Here the screen of the visual display unit is criss-crossed by a lattice of infra-red beams, invisible to the human eye. When a finger is pointed at the text the system detects a disturbance in the infra-red lattice with the same results achieved by a mouse-based system.

More inputting devices

Other alternatives are just beginning to come on to the market. For example, ACT are advertising a personal computer which recognises the voice of the user and will respond to verbal commands for basic functions. However, there is still a long way to go before text can be dictated into a computer and instantly displayed on the VDU.

There is no doubt that voice activation will have a role to

play, but material printed on paper will be around for a long time yet and the real breakthrough will come when there is a viable alternative to keyboards in the form of a cheap and accurate device for reading and inputting hard copy. The technique known as *Optical Character Recognition* (OCR) has been around for some time, as indeed has *Magnetic Character Recognition* (MCR) which is widely used by banks for reading cheque numbers and so on. The difficulty seems to be in finding a system that combines cheapness with accuracy. Until such an alternative becomes freely available the keyboard is really the only viable option for inputting information. One thing is certain, anyone intending to use a computer with the hope of getting the best out of it should really take the trouble to learn to type.

Screening it

The screen is quite simply a device where you can view information stored in the memory of the computer. The jargon for a screen is *visual display unit* or VDU for short. As with the keyboard, the choice of screen is very much tied to the central processor.

There are sometimes options which can make the difference between an adequate and an excellent screen. Perhaps the most obvious is its capacity for being adjusted. Most of the latest screens can be tilted and swivelled to achieve a setting most comfortable for the operator.

You should also be able to adjust the brightness of the text.

The finish of the screen surface should also be considered. Some screens are highly reflective and when the screen is transported from the computer showroom to your office environment you could find operators suffering eye-strain through reflected glare from fluorescent lighting. More than one company has made a useful business out of supplying special polarised filters to fit over the front of VDUs.

Colour

When it comes to screen colour you have an increasing number of choices. The monochrome option usually offers you the opportunity of having text displayed in either green or amber. Opinions as to which is best, that is easy to read, more soothing and so on, vary. It seems to be purely a matter of personal choice.

The one thing to ensure is that the visual display unit is 'high resolution'. This means that you get a much sharper image than you would, say, with an ordinary domestic television receiver. Many of the really small computers do offer the option of using an ordinary television screen for visual display, but this can be a disaster, particularly if you are inputting text through a word processing package. For a start it is unlikely the definition will be good enough to give you a proper 80-column width display — the letters would appear too fuzzy. Second, even at half the width of display, the lack of sharp definition would give rise to eye-strain after prolonged use.

A number of hardware manufacturers offer colour screens as an option with their computer systems. The argument for colour is said to be that it offers greater clarity and more interest for the user. If you plan to use your computer only for accounts and word processing it is hard to see how colour would be a great advantage. Of course, if graphics is the main interest, colour may well come into its own, but in most cases any graphic display will have to be printed out and unless you have a full colour printer (again very expensive) there will be little advantage. A colour display, printing out in black and white, might even prove somewhat misleading. That said, colour screens are gaining ground, particularly for work station type computers such as the One Per Desk from ICL, which is designed for use among middle managers. One can see that the colour screen option will provide scope for 'status enhancement' if nothing else.

Quite often the difference in price between the colour and monochrome option is fairly small, seldom more than a couple of hundred pounds. Colour might well be considered an attractive bonus, but a colour screen in itself will not guarantee a colour display; the software has to be written so that colour will be displayed. Many programs are written so they will work on either colour or monochrome screens — the word processing package Wordstar is one example. Here different colours are used to separate input text from command options. Operators I have talked to who use a colour option seem to have enjoyed the experience. Whether there is any extra efficiency as a result is debatable.

If it is important to involve the eventual user of the computer with the decision over the keyboard, it is vital to do so when it comes to choosing the visual display unit. There are still many misconceptions about computers. One of them is that radiation from visual display units is in some way harmful. It is right that such fears are taken seriously and much research is being carried out into the effects of day-long close proximity to a computer screen. So far there has been little conclusive evidence that VDUs are damaging in the long term; nonetheless there are worries. In the short term operators often complain of headaches and boredom. They work better when given breaks doing alternative work not involving the VDU.

It is only sensible to ensure that the operators are happy with the screens. If they are not, excuses will be found to leave them whenever possible with resultant losses in efficiency. It will be difficult to 'mix and·match' computers with keyboards and screens because they tend all to come as one in a given hardware system. If you have been consulting with staff all the way along the line you should not, at this relatively late stage, find yourself making hardware choices on the basis of cosmetics. Given enough information about the options, the staff themselves will make the right compromises between their comfort and the needs of the business. It cannot be stressed too highly that this is the one area where it is important to get the staff on your side. Other choices are much simpler.

Disk drives

At the moment, business users have little choice but to use floppy disks for storage of information and inputting software (see pages 82–4). Tape cassette systems can be dismissed out of hand — they are just too slow for any kind of efficient business use, although 'floppy tape' systems where tape is run at high speed do have a limited application, primarily in small-scale work station type computers.

As with keyboards and screens, the disk drives themselves are usually dictated by the choice of central processor. In most cases, the disk drives are an integral part of the central processor but many hardware manufacturers are now offering options. The first option is to have just one disk drive.

Disk drives are expensive, so it is tempting to go for just one, thus saving a significant amount on the price of the hardware. Unless you plan to use your computer only sparingly you will find this false economy, especially if you intend to run either powerful programs or use valuable information stored on floppy disk. It is to be presumed that all information is valuable, otherwise you would not be putting it on computer.

You will want, for example, to make back-up copies of your client list or accounts, to be stored in a separate place for calling up in the event of the master copies going astray or being damaged. This is not impossible to achieve with a single disk drive, but it becomes much simpler if you have two. Some software is so arranged that back-up copies are made automatically as you input information. Double disk drive allows you to use one drive as an extra memory, in effect, so that the memory of the central processor is not taken up with the program, leaving no room for the computer to do any 'thinking'. In short, a double disk drive allows you more software options.

Another alternative being offered by hardware manufacturers is that of having a single disk drive backed up by a built-in *hard disk*, often known as a *Winchester disk*. A hard disk is usually built in permanently to the central processor and has greater storage capacity than a floppy disk, usually 10 megabytes (one megabyte is equal to 1,000 kilobytes). It takes one byte to store one letter or number, so imagine what you could store on a hard disk with 10-megabyte capacity — 10 million bytes. The text of several books or some very complicated software.

A hard disk allows you to input several programs into the system to be held on the hard disk and used as necessary. Much more of the memory of the central processor itself is then free to do the 'thinking'. The single floppy disk is used simply to dump information for storage purposes or input information from an outside source. A hardware system with a hard disk and single disk drive will provide most businesses with all the computing power they are ever likely to need.

Although the disk drives are likely to be built into the central processor, it is possible to have them as separate units. This is particularly useful when it comes to upgrading a system. You could, for example, bolt on a hard disk unit or add another disk drive to a single disk drive system. In this way you can expand your computer power with the business. You will, of course, need to check that this option is open to you. Quite often, especially when you are using 8-inch systems, the physical size of the disk drives often makes it more sensible to have them separate from the central processor anyway. This means that the central processor can be placed out of the way — on the floor or on a shelf, for example. The disk drives can then be positioned somewhere convenient for the operator, either on the desk, or quite frequently with 8-inch disks, slung under the desk to one side. Obviously this is a matter for some consideration.

Disk storage

Do not overlook the question of storage of floppy disks. As the business grows, you will acquire a number of them. There could be over a hundred if you take into account software disks as well. It is particularly important to ensure that they are stored safely.

Floppy disks are more susceptible to damage than any other piece of office equipment: just touching the magnetic surface can be enough to corrupt the information held on file. They do not like extremes of temperature and humidity, and any kind of magnetic field can spell disaster. This means the disks shouldn't be allowed near telephones (there's a magnet in the bell). They shouldn't rest on top of a disk drive unit (the motor will have a magnet) or near a TV screen or VDU (the screen gives off magnetic radiation). Even a paper clip can wreak havoc.

One of the chief causes of disk corruption is rough handling. This can happen when disks are in transit between offices. So often floppy disks stored in a box are bent as the operator sorts through them. Fortunately there are special boxes now available to overcome this problem. One of these is the 'SEE 10' which, as its name implies, allows 10 disks to be stored at a time and through an ingenious front opening flap allows the labels on all 10 to be viewed at a time. When the disks are not in use the plastic box is closed to protect them from dust. Proper storage boxes are worth the extra money. Taking into account the keyboard time required to input information, just one disk could represent £1,000-worth of work.

Case study: the second-hand option

Jeremy McLaughlin is based in Kent from where he operates as a business consultant trading as The Company Doctor. He has also been involved in business on his own account. Five years ago he was running his family's wine importing operation with an annual turnover of around £1 million. They, like so many companies of that size, saw computerisation as a way of streamlining their routine business systems, but also in common with other companies, did not have a lot of money to spend. Jeremy McLaughlin looked at what was on offer and plumped for a second-hand system costing then (1981) £7,500.

The company or rather group of companies was involved in a wholesaling operation, processing up to 60 orders a day in relatively high value merchandise, where each unit needed to be accurately accounted for. Furthermore, there were a certain amount of unavoidable 'returns' and 'to follow' situations where merchandise either did not meet specification or was not instantly available in the warehouse. Before the advent of the computer, all of this operation was controlled using mechanical sales and stock ledger systems.

In previous generations a 'steam driven' magnetic card system had been in operation which was kept going well beyond its life expectancy by a conscientious and attentive staff. However, when it came to the point where this system could no longer be serviced, something had to be done and that had also to be something that would not bankrupt the company.

Having looked at a number of the latest machines available at the time we ended up deciding to purchase second-hand hardware together with operating systems, from a small, independent computer company which, while its mainstream activity was selling new computers, often found itself with second-hand equipment taken in as part-exchange.

The price quoted for the equipment, delivery and back-up — around £7,500 — was within our means and offered us more than enough computing power. Looking back, it's fascinating to reflect on how puny the 24K central processor now looks compared to the computing power available just a few years later at a fraction of the price. However, it suited us at the time and, all in all, we thought we had a bargain.

The disadvantage of taking on a second-hand system was that in those days the hardware manufacturers were still grappling with the problem of reducing the overall physical size of their units. The system on offer involved separate free-standing units for both central processor and hard disk drive. These days, for that level of computing power, both would probably be housed together in one much smaller unit. Additionally some of the equipment was quite dated (at the time of the transaction about five years old). The size issue was not a problem as the company had spacious warehouse premises, and was able to accommodate the machinery in its accounts department.

Once the initial problems of coding were overcome the accounts staff warmed to the system which, whatever its drawbacks, to the informed seemed a hundred times better than that to which they had been accustomed. Certain facilities improved productivity immeasurably, notably the production of monthly statements and the production of data at cut-off dates.

Some compromises had to be accepted to keep the software costs within bounds (the software was lifted virtually unchanged from the previous users). This created problems in one area, namely that of returns. The problem arose from the fact that, while wine sales were made in case lots of one dozen units, returns from breakages were inevitably in single bottle units. The rewriting of the program to cope with this contingency was never dealt with satisfactorily, possibly because there was not sufficient motivation on everybody's part, whether salesman or purchaser. The result was that the return of single bottles always called for a fudged adaptation of the main operating system which was never completely successful.

Apart from this minor hiccup, the rest of the system worked without fault for two years until we sold the company. For us it had proved an extremely wise and economical investment. Not only that, had the new management wished, there was infinite potential to expand the system to cope with other business developments.

Chapter 16
Peripherals

Peripheral is the term used by computer people to describe anything that isn't central to the computer operation. From that you should not assume that a peripheral is somehow less important than the rest of the hardware in any computer set-up. Among the devices considered peripheral are *printers* which turn the electronic messages stored within a computer memory into hard copy (printed paper) for all to read, and *modems* which enable computers to talk to others at long distance. Modems have limited applications in the business world except where there is a need to link computers together or access information from a larger computer, but virtually every business computer system will include a printer of some type or another. Choosing the right printer for your particular business application is a crucial decision.

Printers

The majority of business users have to choose between two distinct types of printer: they can either plump for a *dot matrix* or a *daisy wheel* printer. *Thimble* printers operate in the same way as daisy wheels except that the characters are held on a thimble-shaped print head.

There are also *laser printers* which use photocopying techniques and *ink jet printers*, which 'spray' on the type. Such printers are designed for very fast work but at the moment price tends to rule them outside the scope of most businesses.

The dot matrix printer is fast but doesn't normally produce print to the quality of, say, a good electric typewriter. The daisy wheel printer is slow but usually produces finished copy indistinguishable from high quality hand-typed material. In some cases the quality is equal to that produced by typeset printing. The drawback is that daisy wheel printers are generally much more expensive than dot matrix printers.

As its name implies a dot matrix printer uses a series of dots, electronically controlled to print each character on to the paper. This can either be done through an inked ribbon similar to those used on conventional typewriters or directly on to pressure- or heat-sensitive paper. The latter form of dot matrix printer has the advantage of added speed but in practice the copy quality is usually so poor that it is really only useful for printing out data for internal use and such printers find most use in semi-scientific applications where, for example, they might be attached to monitoring equipment requiring some kind of hard copy read-out.

When it comes to using dot matrix printers for business, there really is no other choice but the inked ribbon variety. Speeds of over 100 characters per second can be achieved by many dot matrix printers, but if copy quality is a major concern, do check out every printer under consideration to see that the typeface is acceptable. Some of the more expensive dot matrix printers offer a facility whereby the rate of print can be slowed down and each letter struck twice to create a darker image. Using this *double strike* facility you can achieve copy of near letter quality simply by sacrificing print speed.

Daisy wheel printers work in much the same way as the more recent kinds of electronic typewriter. The letters are held individually on the end of flexible plastic stalks fixed to a central circular core — the flower-head effect created gives rise to the name 'daisy wheel'. As the printer operates, the daisy wheel is rotated so that the correct letter is aligned with the paper and then struck — again, as with a conventional typewriter, through a ribbon. All of this happens faster than the eye can follow, but not that fast. While daisy wheel printers can offer top quality printing they are slow — some print as few as 18 characters a second. This can be a distinct disadvantage when a large amount of work needs to be printed — a mail shot for example. If you have a computer system which doesn't allow other tasks to be carried out while the computer is in printer mode you could end up with a very inefficient set-up.

The obvious answer would be to invest in two printers, one dot matrix, the other daisy wheel, and some businesses do just that. Printers are not cheap. A really good daisy wheel could set you back not far short of £1,000 and it is unlikely you would get an acceptable dot matrix printer for under £200. Because peripherals involve considerable amounts of mechanical technology, it seems unlikely that they will come down further in price as other computer hardware has done.

If you really want to buy two printers, you could be adding another 50 per cent to the price of a smaller computer system costing around £2,500. Choosing between dot matrix and daisy wheel is difficult, and for most businesses it is likely that neither will, in the final analysis, fill the bill perfectly.

Whichever you decide upon, do check that the printer is compatible with your particular hardware and software system. Most of the more expensive printers, whether dot matrix or daisy wheel, can be adjusted through a series of internal switches to work with most of the major hardware systems. There are some, chiefly dot matrix printers, which are specific to one manufacturer's hardware. Some will only work with one kind of software and may require either internal adjustment or connection to the central processor by a special (expensive) cable before it will print.

Once you have arranged for your printer to print on command from your computer system it will behave in different ways depending on its type and the software package in use. For example, dot matrix printers offer far more facilities for making type look different. They can not only print bold, but also enhance a given typeface (make it larger and thicker). Some dot matrix printers can also compress type and even reverse it so that the character appears white on a black background. The latter option is seldom satisfactory as it is difficult to get most printers to print a really dense black background. On the other hand, many dot matrix printers find it difficult to underline text while this is usually no problem for a daisy wheel printer.

Daisy wheel printers, while they can usually type bold, cannot enhance or compress type size. A daisy wheel printer, though, does give you the opportunity of changing typeface in mid-document by instructing the computer to pause at a predetermined point so that you can swap over the daisy wheels. Using the pause command contained in most good word processing software it is also possible to change type colours (by changing the ribbon) within a document, although changing ribbons is easier on some printers than others.

A word on costs. Plastic daisy wheels are available for around £5.00 each; longer lasting metal print wheels cost around £25.00; plastic thimble print heads are around £10.00. Ribbons can cost between £1.50 and £6.00.

Paper feed

Whichever type of printer you opt for, you will also have to consider the paper supply. It is tempting to look upon printers as ordinary typewriters and think only in terms of feeding in paper a sheet at a time. Such is the ease with which you can produce documents through a computer-based word processing program, you will soon find that feeding in single sheets of paper by hand is tedious, time-consuming and, in the long run, impractical. You have two choices: either opt for a printer which has a *tractor feed*, or invest in a separate *sheet feeder*.

Many printers incorporate tractor feeding within the machine itself in the form of sprockets fixed to the platen (roller), designed to fit holes punched along the edges of a continuous run of paper. After printing, the sheets can be separated by tearing along the perforations. The sprocket holes can also be removed leaving sheets which, if they have been perforated with 'clean rip' perforations, look virtually the same as standard cut sheets of paper. I say virtually, as for some reason most tractor feed paper is slightly larger than a standard A4 cut sheet, although usually the same width.

Paper widths can vary so it is as well to check that the sprockets on the printer or tractor feed are adjustable. You may also want to use much wider paper for printing out spreadsheets, for example. Here you will obviously need a double width printer, but if it has built-in tractor feed do check that it can take paper of any width so that it can be used for both financial printing and typing letters.

Another advantage of tractor feeding is that it gives great accuracy when printing large numbers of documents. You can programme the computer to remember how long each sheet of paper is and automatically advance the paper at the end of a page.

Similarly tractor feeds are a boon when it comes to printing address labels. These are usually adhesive and stuck very accurately, either two, three or four abreast, on to a sprocketed sheet. By feeding in details of the label size and spacing you can leave the printer to type literally hundreds of labels with little fear that there will be a slippage and loss of registration during the printing process.

Sheet feeders are designed as an alternative to tractor feeds and while they do not offer the same positioning accuracy as a tractor feed system, they do make it possible to use pre-printed stationery — business letterheads for example. Sheet feeders are expensive — some can cost as much as the printer itself. You will need to justify the extra expense when weighed against the advantages of being able to use pre-printed paper of high quality which is now available for tractor feed. Inevitably any business introducing a computer for the first time is likely to have stationery in stock and it would be useful and economic if it could be used for word processing. There is no reason why this should not be done but do check that your stationery will work with the particular sheet feeder you have in mind. Take some of your existing stationery along to the showroom and insist that it be used for the printing demonstration.

While we are on the subject of stationery, it is possible to have tractor feed paper printed, but you are talking about quite considerable runs before it becomes cost-effective and most businesses getting into computers for the first time are unlikely to want vast stocks of printed stationery. If you are planning a large number of mail shots, for example, it might be worth considering. Many printers with built-in tractor feeds will also take single sheets. If you have to choose between tractor or sheet feeding, most businesses will probably find tractor feeding printers of most use in the first instance.

To sum up, when choosing a printer you will need to consider the following key points:

1. With the market as it is at the moment, realistically you only have a choice between a dot matrix and a daisy wheel printer.
2. Inevitably you will have to compromise between what you want and what each can deliver.
3. If most of your word processing is to be regular correspondence then you probably want a daisy wheel printer.
4. If you are planning a large amount of printing where speed is important then a dot matrix printer is for you.
5. You might be able to get almost letter quality from a dot matrix printer if you pay more and get a printer which has a double strike facility.
6. Whichever printer you choose, check that it is compatible with your existing hardware and software.
7. Think about the implications in terms of the firm's existing stationery. It would be nice to use it up, but not necessarily at the expense of buying a sheet feeder.

8. If you are going to use existing stationery, ask for a test run to check that it will work with a sheet feeder.
9. If you really want both speed and quality, consider buying two printers! It might pay in the long run.

Printout costs

The cost of printouts varies with what you want to include in the cost calculation. Computer paper itself, quality for quality, is more expensive than conventional cut sheets — you could pay anything from £15 to £50 for 2,000 sheets of A4 for use with tractor drive depending on the quality. On straight printing, computer printout costs compare favourably with conventional typewriting. It is worth noting, though, that the ease of printing out on computer inevitably leads to more paper being generated and increased stationery costs.

Modems

A modem is a device which helps one computer speak to another. By computer, we could in this instance be talking about any kind of device from a mainframe to the smallest of micro computers or even a basic telex machine. In essence, a modem turns the electronic signals which are generated within a computer system into a form whereby they can be transmitted accurately and securely. The transmission has to be accurate for obvious reasons and as most business information could, by definition, be of use to someone outside the business, security is a must. Perhaps the earliest form of modem was the famous 'scrambler' used on telephones during the second world war. Conversations are jumbled up, sent down the telephone line, and unscrambled at the other end.

These days modems are designed not so much to jumble up information as simply to encode it in a form that can be easily transmitted, although where security is a high priority, extra circuitry may well be introduced to stop messages between computers being intercepted during transmission.

Increasingly it is not only telephone lines which are being used, but radio links as well. A whole new area is opening up whereby 'satellite' terminals can link into a central computer. By this means it is possible to have salesmen out on the road equipped with a computer terminal in a brief-case so they can instantly check stock availability, using a radio link to get through to their company's central computer.

In the main, there is little opportunity to choose between types of modem; you are very much tied to those which have been specifically developed with your particular hardware system in mind. It is as well to check the flexibility of a particular modem. It is relatively simple for a modem to provide a link with another computer of the same make as yours. You should enquire into its capabilities of talking to other computer systems. This is particularly important if you want to make use of public computer facilities such as Prestel or some of the highly specialised computer databases such as EuroLex — a database which enables lawyers to access case law and precedents throughout the European legal system.

As businesses develop there is no doubt that accessing a relevant database will be increasingly important, particularly as information assumes a greater role in business life. Anyone introducing a computer system to a business needs to be mindful of these developments, otherwise the business could end up with a number of computer terminals unable to interrelate with each other.

In strict hardware terms, a modem consists of a box full of the necessary electronics with links to the central processor and the telephone line. When computers were first linked together, the device employed was an *acoustic coupler* consisting of two rubber cups into which was inserted the handset of a standard telephone. Signals from the central processor were transformed into high pitched tones, transmitted into the microphone end of the handset. Signals sent in the reverse direction would be picked up from the handset ear-piece. While this system worked reasonably well, there was every likelihood of message corruption due to interference on the line. The amount of information that could be sent in a given time was also limited. Acoustic couplers are still used as a cheap alternative to modems which link directly with the telephone line, bypassing the handset. Using advanced technology such systems allow a higher rate of information transmission which can often give real savings in line charges, particularly where data has to be sent over long distances.

To sum up, you will have to give considerable thought to the modem question if you are planning an operation whereby several computers are to be linked together and you may require to import information from other computer systems or databases. If you simply want your computer for accounts or stock control, with little chance of going outside for information, modems will not necessarily concern you. One final thought: if you do have to make decisions on modems, as with other hardware choices do not allow yourself to be bamboozled by talk of *baud rates* (units of signalling speed in telecommunications) and other such jargon. Just check if the modem will do its job. Realistically the only way you can be sure of this is to check with either the hardware salesman or, if you are using one, an independent computer consultant.

Joysticks and light pens

The joystick is generally restricted to the really small home computers. Using a joystick it is possible to control the movement of some predesignated figure or image on the screen and move it about. Joysticks really come into their own for computer-based adventure games and, generally speaking, they have few applications in business, but it is possible to use one to move a cursor or pointer about the screen in much the same way as one would use a mouse. This may be an advantage in some business computer applications, particularly in computer-aided design. If you are considering a joystick for your system, then it is best to get the most expensive available. Joysticks are very cheap anyway and it is not worth saving a few pounds and risking a mechanical failure.

Light pens are normally restricted to specialised business applications such as computer-aided design. Using a light pen it is possible to 'draw' directly on to the computer screen, thereby creating exactly the image you desire. The beauty of the system is that you do not have to be an excellent artist. Once the light pen has allowed you to draw a very rough outline of the object you can then use it to enhance your drawing. With some software programs it is also possible to make fine adjustments to the image via the keyboard.

Light pens are also used to 'pick up' objects from a separate area and place them into a screen configuration. For example, if you were drawing a circuit diagram you might have a facility to pick up graphical representations of resistors or transistors and transfer them to their correct position on the screen using a light pen system. Light pens are also used to pinpoint areas for graph making.

Bar code readers

Most people are familiar with *bar codes* — strips of parallel lines which are to be found on most food packaging and many other items, such as books. Each item is allocated its own unique set of lines or code containing often well over 30 characters.

Such codes can be read by special readers. There are two main types. One is in the form of a wand — similar to a light pen — which is stroked over the bar code. In this way the code is fed into the computer where it is processed and/or stored. Another form of reader, often found in supermarkets, consists of a transparent panel over which the item with the bar code simply has to pass at any angle, to be read by a laser beam and register in the computer.

Bar codes are used in manufacturing to trace the progress of components as they are assembled into larger machines thus making fault finding and rectification much easier. In a retail/wholesale operation bar codes greatly simplify stock control. With bar code input much faster and more accurate than through conventional keyboards their use is increasing in industry, and bar code readers are growing in importance as peripherals.

Future developments

There are many other applications too but we are now getting beyond the software needs of the average business computer user. There will undoubtedly be other peripherals coming on to the market. The big leap forward will be when a cheap Optical Character Recognition (OCR) device is available. Already there is a device selling for around £500 which reads one line at a time.

There is a market too for any device which irons out the differences between various computer systems. As mentioned earlier, already 'smart' cables exist with built-in electronics which enable different hardware to interact with each other, notably printers with central processors. What most computer systems could definitely benefit from is an electronic box of tricks which allowed whole systems to talk to each other. Until such devices become readily available we are stuck with the peripherals we have, but it is as well to remember that while they may be called peripheral, these devices are in most cases central to the whole business operation.

Chapter 17
Installation

You should by now already have given some thought to where your computer is likely to live within your organisation. In the case of smaller systems the likelihood is that you will be buying a self-contained unit that will require nothing more than a suitable power supply.

Power supply

These days, such is the low consumption of computers, virtually any amperage supply will be sufficient to run the machine, although certain types of monitors, notably those with colour, do still have a relatively high current consumption.

Modern computers are less susceptible to fluctuations in power supply than their forerunners. Time was when a slight blip in the voltage would send the computer into paroxysms of confusion with memories being wiped and complicated software programs crashing, that is ceasing to function, in such a way that they needed to be reloaded into the computer. Some computers are still sensitive in this way, but usually most business computer systems are immune to such dangers.

The power supply taken care of, what are the other factors? Generally speaking they fall into two clearly definable areas. The first is the environment that is best for the computer. The second is the environment which suits the business and those who work within it.

The computer's ideal home

Human beings are bad news for computers. Apart from inputting wrong information, they do nasty things to them like spilling coffee on the keyboard, use paper clips to attach notes to the floppy disks and so on. Computers do not like extremes of hot and cold. Strong sunlight can affect them, as can a smoky atmosphere. Most computers would thrive in an air-conditioned, darkened room where people, coffee and paper clips were banned.

The days when computers needed a highly controlled environment are now past, and most people can decide where to site a computer on the basis of their business needs. That is not to say one can ignore the needs of a computer. Problems quite often arise when, for example, a computer is brought in to rationalise stock control.

While the average office environment, say the office of the managing director who will want to access information held on the stock control database, will be relatively friendly to the computer and its hardware, the siting of a computer terminal on the parts counter of a motor agency could well cause difficulties. To a certain extent keyboards can be protected from debris and foreign matter by covering the keys with a specially designed piece of transparent flexible plastic. If the parts department often issues items containing large amounts of metal there could be problems arising from magnetic fields generated by electric motors and the like. Additionally the presence of minute metal particles on the hands of operatives could spell potential disaster. These risks are further magnified if the computer terminal has its own localised disk drive facility.

In the main, these problems tend to arise only where there are specialised computer applications. For the average business computer the problem is not nearly so acute, as most systems will be used in standard office environments. If risk is to be reduced certain office customs and practices will have to be reviewed.

Men and machines

The office is regarded by many people as a home from home. No matter how well planned or designed office developers think their properties are, as soon as real people move in little signs of individuality begin to appear. A pot plant here, a poster there; all the kind of touches that go to make offices more acceptable to the people who have to work in them. While no one would suggest that the advent of the computer should relegate people to the role of extensions to the machines, there are some traditional office activities which will have to be looked at.

So You Think Your Business Needs a Computer?

We are familiar with the situation where the secretary's cheese sandwich sheds half its filling into the typewriter only to reappear as a greasy stain on some important board paper. Because of the very nature of the computer's ability to concentrate so much more into both time and space, the cheese sandwich factor becomes that much more critical. Even morning coffee can be regarded as a threat!

It is the same with smoking. Cigarette smoke will not in itself damage computer hardware but if there are floppy disks around it can create havoc. Just one particle of smoke is several times greater than the microscopic gap between the magnetic surface of the floppy disk and the read/record heads of the disk drive. (For more on the environmental risks to computers see Chapter 3.)

The introduction of computers might well be a heaven-sent opportunity to formulate a tough policy on smoking in the office. Non-smokers are now in the majority and such a policy would probably meet with widespread approval; the smokers themselves might even applaud the move on the grounds that it would serve to help them kick the habit. The overall result could well be a healthier working environment for both computer and people.

People first

So much for making the machines comfortable. What about the people? They have given up smoking, drinking and eating in the office, what are you going to do for them?

The first point to be restated is that if you have left it until the point where you are about to install your computer to involve the staff, you have probably left it too late. By now the people who will work on the computer from day to day should have a fair idea about the hardware and software involved and what it will do for them. They will have formulated opinions about how they would like the system to perform; some may even have ideas about what future tasks they would like to see computerised. At a more basic level you will have given operatives an opportunity to try the hardware for themselves; select the keyboard which suits them; satisfy themselves that the visual display unit is going to tilt and swivel to suit them and that the screen produces text in the right colour and can be adjusted for brightness.

If you have been astute in your consultations you will have avoided references to the computer substituting for any office activity, insisting instead that it is designed to enhance existing operations. The last thing you want to do is give the impression that existing office machinery with which everyone is familiar will go out the door on the eve of the computer being installed. It sounds crazy, but there are many firms, which having taken the advice of an over enthusiastic computer buff, either within the company or employed as an outside consultant, have done just that! Remember how possessive people are about typewriters — many even write their names on them. Despite the fact that modern electric machines of the same make and model tend to be more uniform than their mechanical forebears, I know of several instances where secretaries transferred to another department have taken their own machines with them although there may be a newer version of the same model awaiting them. It is an unwise manager who interferes with that level of feeling between person and machine.

So we have come to the first law of installing a computer:

The computer must be seen to be an addition to rather than a replacement of existing office machinery.

Making room

The first law of computer installation clearly presents problems of space, particularly when office accommodation is at a premium. The only comfort one can give is that if your computer choices have been made wisely your staff will so quickly take to the new machines that it will soon be possible to phase out or reduce the number of older machines and thus save space.

You will have noticed that so far I have been talking about the office as an entity and in terms of seeing computer installation as an office-wide operation. This is deliberate. The chief advantage of the great technological leaps made in the computer world in recent years is that computing power can be put into the hands of many more people.

The last thing you want to do is create another elite within your organisation — that of the specialised computer department. Ask anyone who worked during the sixties and seventies for large firms which had their own separate computer departments (they tended to call them data processing departments in those days). Most seem to have horror stories about how they could never get access to the information they wanted. If they challenged this, the DP manager could always cite pressure of work in the sure knowledge that computers were so specialised no one could disagree with him. Another cry often heard was that data processing departments were all data and no information. Of course, not all DP departments were like this, but the underlying trend was always present by virtue of the very position of the department within the company hierarchy.

Thus we come to the second law of computer installation:

The computer must always be within easy reach of those who need to use it and its information.

Of course that sounds very obvious but once you start to think about it you can soon imagine the conflicts that can arise. Earlier in your computer decision-making process you may have plumped for stand-alone computers (that is, those capable of operating independently) which do specific tasks; one for accounts, another for stock control, separate word processing and so on. You may also have decided that it would help if they were flexible to the extent that, should one piece of hardware go down in accounts, a similar piece could be wheeled in from a word processing operation if there was a pressing need to get some accounting function completed by a certain time. Much of this compatibility is software dependent, but you will have made a conscious decision to go for smaller units which perhaps have the capability of talking to each other or replacing one another.

The alternative is to have some system which works on shared logic. Shared logic is a system where a number of terminals share the same central processor. The terminals cannot operate on their own — they need to access the software loaded into the processor — and are sometimes referred to as 'dumb' terminals.

Increasingly popular, because processor power has become relatively inexpensive, is 'networking' where a number of stand-alone terminals are linked together.

The IMP — the Information Management Processor — from Information Technology Limited (ITL) can run a number of terminals linked together via a central controller the size of a small, two-drawer filing cabinet. IMP terminals are then sited on individual desks within the company. Those terminals may be within the same building or in a number of buildings scattered as far apart as can be linked by telephone line — so in theory they can be anywhere in the world which can be reached by telephone.

Most smaller businesses will probably want to opt for a system that operates within one building, many in just one office. Within one room, linking terminals together should present few problems as long as connecting cables can be placed safely. When it comes to connecting machines in different parts of the building, new wires dedicated to use by the computer only will have to be laid. This need be no more difficult than installing a telephone system. Many modern office blocks are constructed with conduits for computer wiring terminating in special sockets; sometimes the wires themselves are built in. If you are in such a building you will need expert advice on whether existing wires are suitable and in the right place. If you are in an older building there could be difficulties. You may be precluded by the terms of your lease from running cabling visibly along walls and skirtings. In such cases you will have to take it under the floorboards along with the existing power supply wiring — an expensive process both in direct costs and in disruption to the business. Again you will need advice. This is best sought from the supplier of the hardware who should also be asked to quote for installing the necessary wiring. You may also want to get a second or third quote for purposes of comparison. If you find alternative quotes cheaper you may be able to haggle with your hardware supplier. Bear in mind the third law of installation:

Always make the hardware supplier responsible for the installation.

The purchase agreement

The best way of achieving this is to make sure that the whole package — hardware supply, delivery, wiring, installation, hand-over period — is tied up in a precise purchase agreement. The agreement should specify the various items, with a costing for each one. The agreement should also state a time-scale for supply, installation and hand-over. There should be a given start date and a hand-over date. It is only reasonable to allow flexibility to the supplier for 'unforeseen' difficulties, but that should be built into the time-scale stated in the purchase agreement, otherwise you could find yourself waiting longer than you had anticipated. You may like to concentrate the mind of the supplier further by insisting on time penalties for late delivery. In any event be sure that the deal is properly tied up with a purchase agreement specifying an overall price quotation; don't settle for an estimate. A quotation is binding in law, an estimate is not.

All this points to the sense of making the whole project the responsibility of one company. If you go for the option of letting another contractor install the wiring, you could end up with one blaming the other in the event of a system failure. The cost and disruption caused by having to install wiring for networked or shared logic systems tends to add even more force to the argument that individual, stand-alone computers are the answer. There are, though, some half-way houses to be had. Some desk-top computers like the ICL One Per Desk use existing telephone lines to link together. Each OPD has the capability of operating two lines, one for speech, the other for data. There are other systems which use electricity supply ring mains to carry information between terminals. And there are steady advances being made in the field of radio communications between computer terminals which will make expensive wiring a thing of the past.

The final touches

Assuming your hardware supplier has taken on the task of supervising the installation the next step is to look at the ways in which you can make the whole process as painless as possible for your staff.

The first one is to ensure that the general environment is improved with the arrival of the computer. Now is perhaps the time to arrange for the office to be redecorated (but not before any necessary wiring work has been done). As we have mentioned, there is likely to be less space than before because you will not be throwing out existing office equipment. It is easy to be tempted to try to cram the new hardware on to existing desks, but you may actually save space by acquiring purpose-built computer furniture. If it is well designed it will have space not only for the keyboard, central processing unit and screen, but also for separate disk drive units.

Take the advent of the computer as an opportunity for looking at the seating in the office. Some very interesting innovations are being offered which seem to make for much more comfortable operation. Try to get the screen set up in advance of the computer coming on stream proper, so you can see whether glare from existing office lighting will be a problem. You may have to consider investing in anti-glare filters or individual lighting.

By far the most important environmental consideration will be the siting of the printer. All printers are noisy, some more than others. Apart from the level of noise output, quite often the type of noise can be most irritating. In short, printers can cause trouble in a busy office especially if it is open plan. There are two solutions. The first is to enclose the printer in a soundproof box. These are available for virtually all types of printer. The one drawback is that the soundproof box will take up even more room. The alternative is to site the printer in a separate room. This solution is particularly useful if you envisage enough printed output to justify more than one printer. A separate room would have the advantage of containing all the paper overflow that accompanies any printing operation. The same room could also be used for storing paper and accommodating a paper shredder where necessary. It goes without saying that any such room should be near the computer terminals; there is nothing more frustrating than having to climb two flights of stairs to pick up one sheet of printed matter.

The whole purpose of these seemingly cosmetic activities is not to pander to the prejudices of the workforce and in some way 'buy them off' with promises of a new paint scheme and posh chairs. Remember that once the system is up and running, a considerable amount of time will need to be spent at the keyboard, if the best is to be had from any computer system. The idea of these 'cosmetic' suggestions is to ensure that operatives use that time efficiently. If they are fatigued or distressed due to incorrect seating or eye-strain nobody benefits.

Of course, many businesses simply will not feel able to afford such extras, but I cannot stress strongly enough the need for the introduction of computers to be considered as the fundamental step it is. Your office may never be the same again. With any luck you may eventually be able to wave goodbye to some of your older equipment and create more space for the business to expand; this is unlikely to happen if your staff are not happy with the new scheme of things.

Checklist

To sum up, when considering the installation of a computer system evaluate the following:

1. Is there a suitable power supply?
2. Will you need special wiring to interconnect various parts of the system?
3. Does such wiring already exist? Is it suitable?
4. If wiring does not exist, how much will it cost in money and disruption to install?
5. Will your hardware/software supplier undertake responsibility for the installation — in particular the cabling?
6. Is there opportunity (and available cash) to consider redecorating the office and buying extra purpose-built furniture to accommodate the computer?
7. Is this an opportunity to examine the existing seating in the office and replace any which is unsuitable?
8. Check existing office lighting. Will you need to buy filters for the screens?
9. Where will the printers go? Have you budgeted for sound-proofing enclosures? If you have opted for housing them in a separate room is it correctly sited?

Chapter 18
Past, Present, Future?

The world of computers moves so quickly that as soon as you have committed one word on, say, a piece of hardware or range of software to paper, the probability is that what you have written is already out of date. If there is nothing so old as yesterday's newspaper, then computers, particularly those used in business, must run a close second in the senility stakes. But that only applies if we allow ourselves to be sucked into the vortex created by ever louder siren voices exhorting us to buy more, bigger, and better. You can understand the computer salesman's point of view. His success lies in selling more and more boxes of hardware.

Home computers

There is no doubt that some computer markets are reaching saturation. Home computers are an obvious example of this. After an initial boom in both the United States and the UK, interest has waned and in many households the home computer has been consigned to gather dust along with the hula hoop and the skateboard. True, most home computers do have the facility to interact and could form the basis of, for example, home shopping and banking systems, but as the necessary investment for laying cables to every household in order to make such networks viable was not available, they were ahead of their time. When limited to the generation of computer games they were soon tired of. The general public have tried computers and, with some exceptions, decided they are more trouble than they are worth. This will change, no doubt, when a new computer-literate generation comes through.

Business computers

When it comes to business, in some ways it has not been quite so bad, although there are many firms which have tried computers and rejected them. The majority of business users seem content, if not entirely satisfied with the benefits of computerisation. Indeed, many would now find it difficult to function without their computer. For some it has been a long, hard road beset with difficulties, not least of all the insidious pressure to buy more hardware of the wrong kind with little regard for the software. The trouble is that in their efforts to both attract new customers and persuade existing ones to update their installations, the hardware manufacturers are perhaps still being led by their technologists rather than by what the market is demanding. Despite the fact that many of the big hardware manufacturers lay claim to undertaking much market research, something is going wrong somewhere, otherwise why are we continuing to hear computer horror stories?

Bigger, better?

Cast your mind back to the example quoted by Jeremy McLaughlin (page 150) where he brought in a second-hand computer to run invoicing and accounts in his wine business. It all happened as recently as 1980 with a system which had a memory capacity of 24K. Compare that with the huge capacities now available for essentially the same price — capacities large enough to store several books. It is hard to see how further advances in memory capacity would be an advantage for normal business activities.

Storage and retrieval do need looking at: 5¼- and 8-inch floppy disks are rapidly becoming the biggest security liability in a modern computer system. Some improvements are being made with the much stronger outer coverings to be found in the 3½-inch systems used in the Apple and ACT hardware. This will give these manufacturers an extra competitive edge as the battle for hardware customers hots up. No matter how reliable the floppy disk manufacturers make their product, the floppy disk is intrinsically an unsafe storage device.

Friendlier

When it comes to software there is still room for improvement on the business front. With larger memory capacity in the hardware there should be much more room for so called 'friendly' software. It should be possible for software to be positively friendly so that it will not only protect the user from doing something silly and jeopardising large amounts of data, but also offer a helping hand right from the start. So-called 'help' screens should not only serve to get you out of a jam but also take you right through a program, telling you in plain terms how to get the best out of it. In this way it should be possible to present 'self-training' software which, in the absence of a printed manual, would enable the user to access the program as soon as he takes delivery of the disk.

Manuals have become more comprehensible in recent years but there is still some way to go. Where the scale of a system allows, more investment should be made in proper training schemes, so that help is available to new employees directly from the hardware/software suppliers and not just on a 'sitting next to Nellie' basis. A few software houses are looking at video as a way of helping to cut down the training commitment of their staff. One software developer told me how it cost him £800 in training every time he installed one of his accounts packages. It was not so much the direct costs that concerned him but the loss of a skilled programmer on repetitive training for a day at a time when he could be better employed using his talents to develop new programs. For him it was well worth making an investment in a properly produced video training tape. From the client's point of view it was good to know there was ready reference on hand which could be seen rather than merely read.

Some manufacturers have set up user groups to obtain feedback from those with hands-on experience. There should be more of these offering real incentives to group members to offer solutions rather than just criticism. User groups can also be of great help with software. Sadly it is all too often the case that a software developer simply does not have the funds to commit to such an endeavour, so once again the emphasis is on the hardware.

Smarter

In the hardware world it is customary to talk in terms of 'generations' of computers. Soon to arrive will be the fourth and fifth generations. These will bring with them 'artificial intelligence' which, as the phrase implies, is the ability of the computer to 'think for itself'. What level this thinking will be remains to be seen. What is sure is that artificial intelligence may not necessarily be what the business person is looking for from a computer. Business wants accuracy and reliability. For the technologist, artificial intelligence offers more excitement than comes from making existing systems better. We must hope that the quest for such excitement does not distract too many technologists from the advances that need to be made if business is to reap greater rewards from computers.

So what are the advances that will take business down the road to greater efficiency? On the hardware front there is a crying need for a cheap, bolt-on Optical Character Reader. Much inputting time could be saved if such a device was available to scan pages of printed material and set the text in the computer's memory. An OCR would be the real breakthrough in overcoming keyboard phobia. It would also free operatives from much tedious keying in. For this reason alone keyboard alternatives such as mice and touchscreen systems are most attractive.

In the world of software the future must lie in integrated programs running on standardised operating systems. Software integration should be vertical as well as lateral so that, as a company grows, it would be possible to match existing software with larger and faster hardware.

Above all, when it comes to smarter systems, what business sorely needs is real advancement in the field of compatibility. The world of business really is fed up with seeing computer people protecting their own corner, often with seemingly little consideration for the needs of the computer consumer. In an ideal world we would have had standardisation much sooner, but at the moment it seems that the only standardisation some hardware manufacturers will accept is that based on driving the competition out of business. That is certainly not good for the consumer and in the long term it is probably a disadvantage for the computer industry.

Until and unless standardisation is achieved, what business could really do with is a range of devices to enable differing systems to talk to each other. Perhaps the absence of such devices so far is due to the dominance in the hardware market of the large manufacturers. One would like to think it would be possible for a small manufacturer to seize upon this opportunity in much the same way as has been done in the software field.

Over to you

With more complex and sophisticated systems coming on to the market the newcomer to the world of business computers will find it increasingly difficult to make a sound choice. Computers will come and go. Software will become more sophisticated. There will be breakthroughs in technology of deep significance to the business world, and other advances which will only serve to muddy real business objectives. I believe that the nature and level of argument in this book will endure and continue to be relevant as the world of computer technology advances. I sincerely hope that the advice given here will help you to acquire the services of the most independent and objective computer consultant you could possibly wish to have — yourself.

Appendices

1. Where to Go for Advice

There is no shortage of advice in the computer world. The trouble is that much of it comes from vested interests keen on promoting one system over another. There are, though, some independent sources of information. Most local polytechnics and colleges of technology have computer departments and it would be well worth making contact with them in the early stages of making plans for a computer system. Other organisations to try are as follows:

The National Computing Centre
Bracken House, Charles Street, Oxford Road, Manchester M1 7BD; 061-228 6333
They have branches in London, Birmingham, Bristol, Belfast and Glasgow. They also can give you the name of the nearest microsystems Centre. The organisation is backed by the government and industry. You can subscribe to the organisation or simply take advantage of their various advice packages.

Federation of Microsystems Centres
Supported by the Department of Trade and Industry and co-ordinated by the National Computing Centre, there are around 20 specialist microsystems centres around the country. They hold workshops and seminars and their staff offer guidance and hands-on experience free of any commercial pressure.

A full list of microsystems centres is available from the NCC but here is a selection.

Central London
Microsystems Centre, 11 New Fetter Lane, London EC4A 1PU; 01-353 0013

Midlands
Birmingham Microsystems Centre, Birmingham Polytechnic, Wellhead Lane, Perry Bar, Birmingham B42 2TE; 021-356 1008

North West
Merseyside Microsystems Centre, Merseyside Innovation Centre, 131 Mount Pleasant, Liverpool L3 5TF; 051-708 0123

North East
Tyne and Wear Microsystems Centre, Newcastle upon Tyne Polytechnic, Coach Lane Campus, Benton, Newcastle upon Tyne NE7 7XA; 0632 700504

North
West Yorkshire Microsystems Centre, Queenswood House, Beckett Park, Leeds LS6 3QS; 0532 759741

South of England
Dorset Microsystems Centre, Norwich Union House, Christchurch Road, Bournemouth, Dorset BH1 3NG; 0202 26349

South Wales
South Wales Microsystems Centre, Computer Centre, Polytechnic of Wales, Pontypridd, Mid Glamorgan CF37 1DL; 0443 405133

Scotland
Waverley Microsystems Centre, INMAP, 21 Lansdowne Crescent, Edinburgh EH12 5EH; 031-225 3141

Ulster
Ulster Microsystems Centre, Ulster Polytechnic, Shore Road, Newtownabbey, Co Antrim BT37 0QB; 0231 65131 Ext 2675

Information Technology Centres
Manpower Services Commission, Head Office, Moorfoot, Sheffield S1 4PQ; 0742 753275
These are government run — there are over 150 of them throughout Britain. It is best to make an approach at local level through either a Jobcentre or an MSC Training Division office (often the two are in the same building). Their primary aim is to create jobs through helping local businesses.

Association of Professional Computer Consultants
109 Baker Street, London W1M 2BH; 01-267 7144
They can give you names of independent computer consultants.

Computing Services Association
Hanover House, 73-74 High Holborn, London WC1V 6LE; 01-405 3161
They represent more than 80 per cent of computer service organisations in UK. They can advise on consultancy and on purchase agreements with computer suppliers.

Small Firms Advisory Service
Ebury Bridge House, 2-18 Ebury Bridge Road, London SW1W 8QD; 01-730 8451, or dial the operator on 100 and ask for Freefone Enterprise to be put in touch with your nearest office.

Run by the Department of Employment, this is a network of advice centres covering 12 regions. Initial advice from independent counsellors is free. The same services are offered by the development agencies in Scotland, Wales and Northern Ireland:

Scottish Development Agency, 120 Bothwell Street, Glasgow G2 7JP; 041-248 2700

(Small Businesses Division), 102 Telford Road, Edinburgh EH4 2NP; 031-343 1911

Welsh Development Agency, Treforest Industrial Estate, Pontypridd, Mid Glamorgan CF37 5UT; 044-385 2666

Northern Ireland Development Agency, 100 Belfast Road, Hollywood, County Down; 02317 4232.

2. The Data Protection Act

Any business that holds records of personal data on individuals in computer files is required to register immediately with:

The Data Protection Registrar
Springfield House
Water Lane
Wilmslow
Cheshire SK9 5AX; 0625 535777 for enquiries.

Files on individuals already in existence should have been registered by 11 May 1986.

3. Glossary

Acoustic coupler. A device into which a telephone handset is placed to enable computer information to be sent down a telephone line. Must be used in conjunction with a *Modem*.

Back up. The term used to describe the copying of disks as a safety precaution against information being lost through accidental erasure. Some computer systems do this automatically, others rely on the user to 'back up' at regular intervals.

Bar codes. A series of lines of varying thicknesses, printed very close to each other which can be 'read' by stroking a special wand over the code. Useful where keyboard entry is impractical or where high speed entry of information is needed, eg a factory shop floor or supermarket.

BASIC. Acronym for Beginner's All-purpose Symbolic Instruction Code. A computer language commonly used in micro computers. Using BASIC most people find it relatively simple to write or amend their own programs.

Bespoke. A computer program written especially to fit your business needs.

Bit. The basic unit of computer capacity. It takes eight bits to make one *Byte* — the amount of computer space required to hold one character.

Bug. An error in either the software or hardware of a computer system.

Bureau. An agency set up to offer computer services to business. Bureaux often offer access to more powerful computers or to specialist systems on a time sharing basis.

Byte. A measure of computer capacity equivalent to eight *Bits*. One byte represents one character on a keyboard. The capacity of a computer system is measured in *Kilobytes* (thousands of bytes) or *Megabytes* (millions of bytes).

Cartridge. Device which plugs into a computer system, containing either a software program or in some cases extra computer capacity for storing information.

Cassette. Identical to conventional audio cassettes and used for storing information or programs. The use of cassettes is slow and generally considered impractical for business applications. Some specialist cassettes which are faster than conventional cassettes are used in computers such as the Sinclair QL.

Central Processing Unit. The 'brain' of the computer system where information is handled and sorted.

COBOL. Acronym for Common Business Orientated Language. A high level programming language, it uses terms which are related to ordinary English words.

Compatibility. The ease with which two computer devices can be used in conjunction with each other. Checking that all links in the computer 'chain', both hardware and software, are compatible is essential when putting a system together.

Computer-aided design. The use of computers to aid design by the use of computer graphics, modelling, analysis and simulation.

Computer language. A language used to feed instructions into a computer.

Concurrency. The ability of a computer system to handle more than one thing at a time, either perform several tasks (*Multi tasking*) or allow more than one person to use the system (*Multi user*).

CPS. Characters per second — a measure of printer speed.

Crash. What happens when a program refuses to continue; it usually means that the program has to be reloaded, often with the loss of work in progress unless it has been saved as a precautionary measure.

Cursor. A light indicator on a visual display unit.

Daisy wheel. The name given to printers which 'stamp' letters on to a page from an interchangeable plastic wheel. Daisy wheel printers give a high quality finish but are generally slow.

Database. A large amount of data held in a computer system which can be accessed and sorted in a number of ways. Useful for maintaining mailing lists, customer accounts and so on.

Debug. To remove mistakes.

Directory. List of contents on a floppy disk.

Disk drive. A device into which a floppy disk is inserted; it can read the content of the disk and record or write new information on to the disk.

Documentation. Printed instructions which should accompany all hardware and software. Good documentation is essential if you are to get the best from your system.

Dot matrix. A printer which forms images from a series of dots. Such images can be graphics or text. Dot matrix printers are fast but they often sacrifice quality although this can be improved by using a 'double strike' mode where available.

Double strike. Where each character is in effect printed over twice, enhancing the finished look of the printed material.

Enter. The act of putting information into a computer system.

Firmware. A cross between hardware and software usually in the form of instructions held on silicon chips and built into the computer system, although it is capable of being removed or replaced.

Floppy disk. A magnetic disk, usually between 3½ and 8 inches in diameter, which holds computerised information.

Format. The organisation of data in a predetermined order. A new disk has to be 'formatted' before it can be used with the computer system in question. The word is also used in word processing to describe the appearance of the printed page.

FORTRAN. An abbreviation for 'formula translations', a computer language used for scientific and mathematical programming.

Function keys. Special keys which perform often quite complicated sets of instructions at the touch of just one button. Some keyboards, as in the case of word processors, have function keys for specific tasks such as INSERT and DELETE. In other cases function keys can be altered to suit individual needs.

Handshake. The means by which two devices in a computer system 'talk' to each other.

Hard disk. A magnetic disk in a sealed unit (often within the central processor) with very high storage capacity. Sometimes known as 'Winchester disks'.

Hardware. The various pieces of equipment, central processor, keyboard, printer etc, which make up the computer system.

Icon. A picture or diagram displayed on the screen which represents a function, eg a pencil invites the user to 'draw' a picture, a filing cabinet represents the function for saving a file.

Interface. The point at which two devices in the computer system meet.

Justify. A term used in word processing to describe the lining up of a text so that all the lines are of the same length and there is no ragged edge on the right-hand side of the page as found with ordinary typing.

Keyboard. The means by which information and commands are given to the computer system.

Kilobyte. A thousand bytes, often abbreviated to K.

Laser printer. A high speed, high quality and comparatively high priced printer which uses laser light technology.

Load. To input a program into the computer system.

Magnetic character recognition. Means by which the computer, through a special scanning device, recognises characters printed in magnetic ink. Most commonly used by banks on cheques.

Mail merge. A means by which a standard letter can be customised to a mailing list for mailshots, circulars etc.

Mainframe. A large high capacity computer capable of undertaking highly complex computing tasks and carrying them out in a relatively short space of time.

Maltron. A special keyboard where the keys are laid out according to their frequency of use as opposed to the QWERTY keyboard which was originally designed to prevent frequently used keys sticking.

Megabyte. One million bytes. Often abbreviated to Mb.

Modem. A device enabling computer information to be sent down a telephone line. A modem is required at each end of the line to encode and decode the signals.

Monitor. A screen on which computer information is displayed.

Mouse. A small device which is rolled around the desk top to control the movement of the cursor on the display screen (usually displayed as an arrow). When the arrow is pointing at the required function on the screen a button on the top of the mouse is pressed and the function implemented. A mouse is very useful in conjunction with some graphics packages. It has limited use with other computer functions such as word processing.

Multi tasking. The ability of a computer system to perform a number of operations at the same time.

Multi user. The ability of the computer to allow more than one person to use it simultaneously.

Networking. The linking together of several computers, either within one office or one building (Local Area Network System or LANS) or over larger distances (Wide Area Network System or WANS).

Operating system. The means by which a computer system carries out its routine functions. With most systems suitable for business use the operating system has to be loaded into the computer before any applications software can be loaded and run.

Optical character recognition. A device which scans a printed page and inputs the text into the computer system so it can be displayed on a monitor ready for editing in the normal way.

PASCAL. A computer language used for systems programming.

Peripheral. Any piece of hardware which is not the central processing unit of the computer system, eg keyboards, printers.

Pixels. Tiny spaces on a monitor which make up a graphic image. The more pixels per square inch, the clearer the image.

Program. A series of instructions which tell the computer system to perform a variety of functions.

RAM. Random Access Memory — space on silicon chips within the central processor where information is stored and accessed at random. Such information is lost when the computer is switched off.

ROM. Read Only Memory — silicon chips within the central processor which store permanently instructions for the operating of the computer system. These are not erased when the computer is switched off.

Scroll. Word processing term to describe the rolling up or down of a page of text on the screen.

Shared logic. A system in which intelligence is shared between items of hardware, as in word processing systems working from the same central processing unit.

Software. Information in computer language which instructs the computer system on how to operate (operating software) and perform a variety of tasks (applications software).

Unix. A system of operating software of great significance to business users. It enables computer systems to undertake a number of functions at the same time (multi tasking) and be used by more than one person simultaneously (multi user).

VDU. Visual Display Unit — the screen on which computer information is displayed.

Winchester disk. Another name for hard disk.

Word processing. Sophisticated system for typing, editing, storing and printing text. A must for any business which sends out lots of printed circulars, catalogues etc.

Work station. A terminal with access to computer facilities.

Index

Accounts 12-13, 43
Accounts packages 108-15
   allowing for growth 113-14
   hardware selection 113
   multi-user 114
   security aspects 114
   selection criteria 112-15
Acoustic couplers 159
Acoustic hoods 41
Artificial intelligence 174
Association of Professional Computer Consultants 180

Back-up 43, 44, 49, 69, 149
Balance sheet 110
Bar charts 125
Bar code readers 161
BASIC 23, 74
Block ranging 101
Bold type 101
British Telecom 'Gold' system 133
Bugs 43
Business computers, future developments 171-5
Bytes 140
   definition 53

Carriage return 103
Cash flow 13, 91
Central processor 140-41
   capacity 140-41
   concurrency 141-2
   expandability 142-3
   selection criteria 143
Centring 104
Cigarette smoke 164
COBOL 23, 74
Compatibility problems 45, 74-6, 101, 133, 159, 161, 174
Competition 53
Computer applications, checklist 18
Computer contract 59-60
Computer department 22

Computer desks 41
Computer disasters 25, 35
Computer furniture 41
Computer installation, *see* Installation
Computer languages 23, 74
Computer literacy 22-5, 29, 30, 34
Computer operator:
   how many 24
   knowledge needed by 23
   who? 21-30
Computer program 43
Computer program crashes 43
Computer salesman 48-60
   assessment of 55
   visit by 56
Computer specialists 50
Computer stationery 41-2
Computer terminals, location 40
Computing Services Association 180
Concurrency 141-2
Consultation:
   costs 35
   lead time for 27
   need for 25-7
   time required 27-9
   who to involve in 28-9
   see also Software consultants
Continuous stationery 41
Copyright, software 72-3
Costs 31-47
   floppy disks 84
   maintenance 76-8
   messaging systems 134
   microcassettes 84
   printers 154-5
   printout 158
   software 33, 72-4, 88-90
   software consultants 64, 71, 79
   software development 71
   training 76-8, 173
CP/M 75

Index

Credit control 13
Cursor movement 86

Daisy wheel printers 102, 153-5
Data input 43
Data processing 43
Data Protection Act 182
Data storage 40
Databases 18
   capacity of 118
   definition 117
   exploring potential of 120
   fields 119
   formatting entries 118-20
   function of 17
   inputting limitations 120
   key fields 119
   power claims 117
   printed data 120
   requirements for using 117-18
Dealer empathy 51
Dealer selection 51-2
Dealership networks 54, 59
Debugging 58
Delivery dates 58
Disk capacity 75, 83
Disk corruption 150
Disk drives 44, 83, 85, 148-50
   single *v* double 148-9
   see also Hard disks
Disk storage 150
Documentation 79, 85-8
Dot matrix printers 101, 153-4
Dumb terminals 46

Easy Script 99, 100
80-column display 99
Envelopes 42
Estimate 57

Fast formatting 100-101
Fears 18-20, 26
Federation of Microsystems Centres 179-80
Filing 17, 116-24
   see also Databases
Financial accounting 13, 18
Financial benefits 36
Financial controls 108
Financial planning 13, 14, 18
Floppy disks 40, 43, 61-2, 75, 82-4, 98, 148, 150
   costs 84

security 172
see also Disk capacity, Disk drives, Disk storage
FORTRAN 23, 74
40-column display 100

Games-based computers 48
Graphics 125-8
   alternative representations 126
   colour use 127
   image quality 127-8
   importing information 126
   software packages 126-7
Guarantees 43, 59

Hands-on experience 57
Hard copy 41
Hard disks 76, 149-50
Hardware 139-52
   accounts packages 113
   case study 150-52
   comparing systems 53
   costs 33
   definition 31, 139
   future developments 173-4
   matching to software 36-40
   second-hand 115, 150-52
   selection criteria 74
      case study 79-81
Help screens 86, 104-5
High street retailers 48-51
Home computers 171
Humidity 40
Hunt facility 102-3

IBM PC 97
ICL 132
Icons 145
IMP (Information Management Processor) 131-2
Information Management Processor (IMP) 166
Information storage 17, 43, 116, 148
Information Technology Centres 180
Information Technology Limited 131
Ink jet printers 153
Inputting devices 145-6
Installation 162-70
   approaches to 28
   checklist 170
   environmental hazards 162-4

189

first law of 165
general environment 168
modular approach 40
and office layout 168-70
planning 58
requirements 40
second law of 166
staff reactions 164-5
supervising 168
third law of 167
unforeseen difficulties 168
Insurance 44
Invoicing 108-10

Joysticks 160

Keyboard phobia 16
Keyboard skills 19
Keyboards 143-5
Kilobytes 53, 75, 140

Labels and label printing 17, 42, 120, 156
Laser printers 153
Letters 15, 17, 42, 99
    filing 120
Licensing agreements 88
Light pens 160
Loss of data 43-4

Magnetic character recognition (MCR) 146
Mainframe computers 139
Maintenance 76-8
Maintenance contract 42-3
Maintenance costs 46
Malfunction 44
Maltron keyboard 144
Management information 39
Manuals 62, 86, 173
    appendices 87-8
    programming section 87
    reference use 86
Memory 53
Menu driven programs 85
Messaging systems 129-35
    compatibility problems 133
    costs 134
    limitations 133
    multiple access 130
    potential for increasing efficiency 133
    priority levels 129

smart systems 133
via telephone lines 132-4
within the company 129-32
Micro computers 139-40
Microcassettes 84
Microdrives 84
MicroWriter 144
Mini computers 139
Modems 158-60
    baud rates 160
    compatibility problems 159
    definition of 158
    description of 159
    types of 159
Mouse 145
MS/DOS 75
Mystique 19

National Computing Centre 179
Near letter quality 102
Networked system 58
Noise effects 41
Nominal ledger 110
Number pad 144

One Per Desk 84, 132-4, 147, 168
Operating systems 75
Optical character recognition (OCR) 146, 161, 174

Pagination 104
Paper consumption 41
Paper wastage 41-2
Paperless office 41
Parkinson's Law 17
PASCAL 23, 74
PAYE 122, 123
Payroll packages 122-4
    future trends 124
    keeping up to date 122-3
    maintenance contract 123
    running time 123-4
    setting-up time 124
Pegasus 96
Peripherals 153-61
    compatibility problems 161
    future developments 161
Personalised letters 17
Planning for the future 44-5
Polymedia, case study 46-7
Portable computer 24
Power supply 162
    failure of 44

So You Think Your Business Needs a Computer?

Stock purchases 110
Storage 82-5
Success rates 12
Systems analyst 36

Tape cassette systems 148
Telephone links 58
Telex 45, 47
Thimble printers 153
Time investment 34-6
Time-scale estimate 57
Touchscreen system 145
Trades unions 26
Training 19, 34-5, 47, 56, 59, 76-8
   case study 30
   costs 173
Trial balance 110
Typefaces 102

VDU, *see* Visual display unit

VisiCalc 93
Visual display unit (VDU) 146-8
   see also Screen colour section
Voice activation 145-6

Wages, *see* Payroll packages
Winchester disk 149
Windowing 93
Word frequency 107
Word length 107
Word processing 15, 18
   advantages of 15
   participants 16
   potential of 15
   secret of 15
   what it can do 15
Word processing packages 98-107
Word processor 46
Wordstar 96
Wordwrap 103-4

Index

Price-lists 99
Print and edit simultaneously 100
Printers 41, 87, 97, 101-2, 127, 153-8
   costs 154-5
   paper feed 156
   paper widths 156
   selection criteria 157-8
   sheet feed 156, 157
   siting 169
   soundproofing 169
   tractor feed 156, 157
Printout costs 158
Program registration 89
Programming 23
Programming sections, manuals 87
Purchase agreement 167-8

QL computer 84
Quality circles 29
Questions to ask the dealer 52
QWERTY keyboard 143-5

RAM (Random access memory) 141
Random access memory (RAM) 141
Read only memory (ROM) 85, 141
Reversing out text 101
Ribbons 42
Right edge justification 104
RJL Software 136-8
ROM (Read only memory) 85, 141

Sales 108-10
Sales ledger 110
Sales resistance 32
Sales staff 24
Satellite terminals 46, 158
Satisfied customers 54, 55
Screen colour selection 146-8
Search and replace 103
Security aspects, accounts packages 114
Shame factor 19
Shift keys 144
Simultaneous print and edit 100
Small Firms Advisory Service 180-81
Software 61-81
   after-sales service 89
   bundling 90, 135
   case study 136-8
   copyright 72-3

costs 33, 72-4, 88-90
definition 32-4, 61
development 33
future developments 172-3
matching to hardware 36-40
modification 68, 73
off-the-peg 34, 67-8, 71, 72
second-hand 115
selection 33, 54, 59
selection before hardware 61
selection criteria, case study 79-81
specialist packages 135-6
see also Accounts packages; Databases; Graphics; Payroll packages; Spreadsheets; Word processing packages
Software consultants:
   alternatives to 67-8
   business 65-6
   competition between 69
   cost aspects 64, 71, 79
   ideal 64, 70
   long-term view 78-9
   need for 67-8
   one-man band 62-5
   recommendations 66-7
   role of 62
   selection criteria 68-70
   student 63-4
   types of 62-5
Software development 45, 53-4
   cost aspects 71
Software development houses 68
Software/hardware combinations 74-6
Solicitors 16
Specialist dealers 50, 51
Specification 57, 58
Spell checkers 105-7
Spreadsheets 14, 91-7
   case study 96-7
   operation 95
   other uses for 95-6
   packages available 91-4
   software selection 94
   What if? exercises 94
Staff morale 58
Staff reductions 15
Standard letters 15
Status line 100
Stock control 13, 18, 24, 58, 110-12